West Seven Stars and Beyond

Preserving Local History

West Seven Stars and Beyond

Preserving Local History

Clyde Scheib

Table of Contents

Foreword

Introduction

Chapter 1. Brief History of Kimberton   •   1
Chapter 2. West on Seven Stars   •   31
Chapter 3. Parker Ford Village   •   81
Chapter 4. Living with Sowbelly   •   115
Chapter 5. My One Room Schoolhouse •   147
Chapter 6. Underground Railroad   •   181
Chapter 7. Bonnie Brae Park   •   199
Chapter 8. Scheib Genealogy   •   209
Chapter 9. Farming Life   •   219
Chapter 10. Two Forgotten Names   •   229
Chapter 11. Unknown Soldiers   •   247

Appendix   •   257

Bibliography   •   293

Acknowledgments   •   295

Endnotes   •   297

Foreword

One winter night I passed a group of people lining the road with luminaries leading to the Kennedy Covered Bridge. When I pulled over to assist, I learned Clyde and Alda Scheib were the organizers representing the Friends of the Covered Bridge. I soon became part of this holiday tradition.

During the summer of 2019, we started collaborating for fun about local history, where each week, Clyde reiterated stories about the area I am sure he has told numerous times before. Sitting on the back porch, they all started the same way; Clyde augmenting his dialogue with handwritten notes, vintage photographs, reference books, articles and bits and pieces from an endless drawer somewhere in his house. I remember our first discussion was a historical village with a revolutionary era tavern, canal and several aqueducts. On one occasion, Clyde said, "Get in the car" and we toured the Parker Ford historical village, where a new riverside park was being planned. Clyde ended up sketching the historical landmarks in the village which I shared with the task force creating the plan.

On several car trips, the landmarks were only a ruin from a bygone era, but Clyde saw it differently, he saw the past as functioning today and described it like a time traveller emissary.

During that summer, I documented Clyde's historical perspectives as he shared his lifetime of research materials. Now, Clyde shares the results of this effort with you.

Brian Wilde
East Vincent Township
Chester County, Pennsylvania

Introduction

The reason I created this book was to share the history of the landmarks closest to me to allow future generations to understand our roots and the conditions in which our forefathers lived. The second reason is to preserve this history in a format that will stand the tests of time and can be shared, which is in book format on the internet site Amazon.com.

I have observed and am most knowledgable of the landmarks closest to the road where I live, which is West Seven Stars Road. Outside my window, I see the bygone 19th century railroad line called the Sowbelly Railroad. All the early railroads played an import part in our nations industrial development. Down the road is the century old Kennedy Covered Bridge which crosses the French Creek, allowing local farmers access to trade markets. These are a few of the landmarks written in the following pages.

I live close to the villages of Kimberton and Parker Ford where George Washington stopped in 1777. I've always enjoyed telling people about our founding fathers influence in the area and the military endeavors in the fight for independence from the British.

Much of the information came from my personal files collected over the years and the interaction I had with a select group of people and organizations. (See Acknowledgements)

For this I am grateful to share with others.

Clyde Scheib
Kimberton, Pennsylvania

"Liberty, when it begins to take root, is a plant of rapid growth."
George Washington

"There is music in the rattle
Of the tinkling wheat that falls,
In the hopper, as the miller
Stops to heed the gristman's calls."

Sarah L. Oberholtzer
At the Old Mill 1873

"The more land we win, the weaker our army gets in the field."

British Officer
Revolutionary War

Chapter 1. Brief History of Kimberton, Pennsylvania

Kimberton Village circa 1835 [1]

I don't consider myself a historian -- I'm a dairy farmer on a farm one mile west of Kimberton on a farm settled in 1712 by Jonathan Rogers. The seventy years that I have driven through the main village intersection, I can recall the many stories my father told me in tidbits about Kimberton.

Kimberton Country House also known as the Kimberton Inn.

Kimberton Country House is a well known Inn but in the 1930s and 1940s this was not the place to be. Nice people didn't go here. Saturday night was the big night in the bar room with 10 to 12 patrons. Some of the patrons were Charles Shinehouse, local barber from whom you were lucky to get an even haircut.

Main intersection of Kimberton, showing Kimberton Country House.

Benny James, was the local auctioneer who would complete a sale once he had a couple beers. Newton Davis and his wife Erma were innkeepers. Newton Davis sold cattle and horses in the barn near the Inn. He always had dinner for buyers before sales in the Hotel. Erma Sturgis Davis was a seamstress who had a shop on the second floor of the hotel. She also made house calls to her customer's homes for fittings. The Hotel was closed from 1929 to 1932 during Prohibition.

Kimberton resides in East Pikeland Township named after James Pike from Cork, Ireland. It was part of the 30,000 acres adjoining Vincent Township. It was deeded from William Penn to Sir Matthew Vincent, Dr. Daniel Cox and Major Robert Thompson. They formed the Mediterranean Sea Company. William Penn did not sign the deeds so his heirs had a 100 year dispute. A sheriff sale of outlandish proportion in 1789 put Pike's land comprising 10,116 acres into the hands of the highest bidder. As a consequence, 115 landowners who were already settled lost their titles although they were later restored.

Pikeland Meeting House

You would say that Kimberton begins on a rise on the south side of the village. In 1758, nine Quaker families applied for a petition to the Goshen Friends Meeting to establish a place of worship. A petition was granted and Pikeland Friends Meeting House and cemetery was established. Regular services began on schedule in a big log cabin.

Pikeland Meeting Cemetery

Kimberton Friends was established August 14, 1758 with eleven families.[2] It had dwindled by 1870 to so few in number that it was decided to close the Meeting and return its communicants to the Uwchlan Meeting. The original hillside site of the Pikeland Preparatory Meeting was located south of the present jointure of Route 113 and Hare's Hill Road. The Meetinghouse burned in 1802 and was immediately rebuilt on the same site. It served the Friends until 1818 when Emmor Kimber, a Friend, offered a piece of his Boarding School property. The congregation had weakened by deaths, departures and disinterest and needed something to rejuvenate activity.[3]

Also, Kimber realized the advertising value of an advantageously situated Meeting within close proximity to his school. The old unused Meeting

House and carriage sheds, with their burial ground, stood on the hillside site until some time after 1861 according to minutes of the organization. From 1819 until 1870, the Meetings were held in Kimber's church beside the Boarding School.[4]

After Kimber died in 1850, the Meeting again weakened and in 1869, the trustees decided to sell the building and lot. The earliest of our deeds relates that permission to sell had to be secured from the Commonwealth by an act of Legislature. This was done on March 12, 1869. On April 5, 1870, the Trustees of Kimberton Friends Meeting: Morris Fussell, M.D., Joshua Pierce West, both of West Vincent Township, and George L. Maris of West Chester, sold the building and lot to a group of five purchasers for $640. The five were Samuel Bartlett, farmer and miller, Ann D. Maris, wife of Norris Maris; John Reese, of Phoenixville and owner of land in Kimberton; Albert King, farmer of East Pikeland Township; and Ell Huzzard, proprietor of the Kimberton Hotel.[5] On April 2, 1874 the church building and lot were conveyed from Reese, Bartlett, Huzzard and Tyson to "The Minister, Trustees, Elders and Deacons of the German Lutheran Congregation worshipping at the Church called St. Peters in Pikeland Township." The Lutherans agreed to pay $1,750.

The Sign of the Bear Tavern

Among the 115 landowners was George Chrisman, an innkeeper, who in 1791 held title to 227 acres in Pikeland Township which encompassed the future village. Chrisman's home was on the northwest corner of the crossroad and in 1768 he petitioned for a public entertainment license. This became known as the "Sign of the Bear."

Sign of the Bear Inn in 1909.

During his proprietorship, Chrisman erected on his property in 1796 a gristmill and merchant mill. When Chrisman died in 1812 his sons sold the property to John Snyder. Three years later he advertised a valuable plantation and tavern on 260 acres comprised of a large two-story house, two tenant houses, one merchant mill, one saw mill, a complete dam, one spring house, a limestone quarry and kiln.

Sign of the Bear Tavern vintage photo.

Sign of the Bear Tavern modern photo.

General Washington marched his 6,000 troops by the door of the Sign of the Bear Tavern to Nutt Road in Phoenixville, on his way to Coventryville, Warwick and Reading Furnaces. The army was a total of 3-1/2 miles in length. The Chrisman Mill was probably the first impetus beyond that of individual farmers' operations that brought importance to the crossroads which for many years was the village of Kimberton. The mill was not the first mill in the area, the Prizer Mill preceding it.

Prizer Mill with flour loaded on trucks in Kimberton, Pennsylvania. c. 1930

Prizer Mill remnants today.

Chrisman Mill was a large mill for the date, and probably incorporated new milling techniques designed by Oliver Evans and popularized in his 1795 book, "The Complete Millwright".

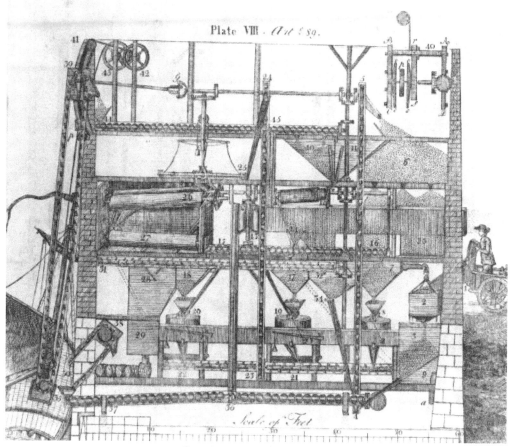

Design of a Grist Mill[3]

Chrisman built a dam, still in evidence, on Royal Spring above the present lower dam, and dug a raceway that crossed Kimberton Road on the later Boarding School grounds. The millrace had an 18' head and fall which turned two 18' overshot water wheels. Three pairs of bur stones ground the grist. The importance of the mill is further seen by the interest it supported in later millers. Never without a miller, the mill operated continuously through the 19th century into the 20th, closing in 1938. Its last owner operator was Sylvester H. Pennypacker. It operated as a store through 1939-1940 and today serves as the Kimberton Post Office.

Kimberton Post Office. (formerly Chrisman Mill)

Emmor Kimber (1775-1850)

In 1817 the entire property was sold to a Quaker school master named Emmor Kimber. Adding to the two story house, Kimber opened French Creek Boarding School for Girls in 1818. In 1820 Kimber as local postmaster, opened a post office and a general merchandise store in what had been the Sign of the Bear Tavern. Two years later, one of the tenant houses was made into a tavern house operated by William Rogers. Rogers called his establishment the Boarding School Inn.

Kimber Hall

The Boarding School became well-known for Greek, Latin, the arts, drawing, painting, etc. Rogers conducted the school for 30 years with the assistance of his wife and daughters. The Kimber family had a total of 11 children. Abigail, 14 years old, Gertrude (age unknown) and Martha Kimber were teachers. Boarding school and tuition was $75/year. The summer term went from May to October and winter term was from November to April. The stage travelled every day from Phoenixville to Kimberton and carriages were for hire at Phoenixville Hotel and Kimberton Boarding School Inn. Laundry items were charged at $.37/ dozen. Students brought a wash basin and towels for their own use. The name of the scholars in winter term of 1840 were Jane Anna Brooke, daughter of Charles Brooke, owner of Hibernia Iron Works (now Lukens Steel); Mary Potts, daughter of Henry Potts (Pottstown Iron Works); Sally Rutter, daughter of John Rutter (Pottstown Iron Works); Elizabeth Whittaker, daughter of the owner of the Phoenixville Iron Works. Students were also from Wilmington and Baltimore. The school closed in 1848.

Gertrude, the youngest of Emmor Kimber's five daughters who taught in the school fell in love with a romantic and penniless abolitionist by the name of Charles Burleigh. Kimber liked Burleigh, but not wanting a wandering life for his daughter, forbade the marriage. Gertrude went on a hunger strike and wept on the Meeting House steps, (the Kimberton Lutheran Church), until the wee hours of the morning. This was more than Dad could bear and he gave in. The couple were married and lived happily ever after to the joy of the 40 pupils of the school.

Kimberton Lutheran Church.

Underground Railroad

Emmor Kimber was one of the links of the Underground Railroad in Chester County. Here, 9,000 fugitives passed through Chester County in those years. John Vickers, a Quaker in Lionville, (where the Vickers Tavern now exists), received the fugitives. Loads of six or seven slaves were brought in the middle of the night from other stations. Women always cheerfully rose and prepared a good meal for them. The fugitives were then hid around the house and surrounding buildings. The next night they were transported to Kimberton Boarding School. Here they were also fed, clothed and hid until transported to another Quaker, Ezra Pennypacker of Phoenixville. From there they were sent to Philadelphia, Norristown, Quakertown or Reading. John Vickers would sometimes give them a slip of paper with the words "Thy Friend Pot" which referred to his occupation as a potter.

In between fugitives, the women would collect clothing from area Quakers, sew, prepare food for the next arrivals on their way to freedom. When they were sick or weary from traveling they were taken to the Lewis family west of Kimberton. While they were staying there, they would sometimes work at the neighborhood farms. Money was also collected from other Quakers for railroad fare to Canada. The fugitives were dressed in better clothing and taken to the railroad station in Parker Ford. There they usually bought tickets in the late afternoon when the sun was in the ticket agent's eyes and he couldn't distinguish what color they were... or maybe he looked the other way.

In 1780, Quakers influenced others to abolish slavery. They formed anti-slavery societies. All Quakers were not sympathetic to this Underground Railroad movement since it sometimes involved violence and Quakers are a peace-loving people. Some Friends started their own meeting. In 1850 the U.S. Congress passed an anti-fugitive law which meant that it was unlawful to hide or steal anyone's property. The fine was $1000 and

6 months in jail. All the owner needed was one witness and he could press charges for someone harboring his property (slave).

For more details on the Underground Railroad, see Chapter 6.

Kimberton Church

On May 20, 1872, a committee of three men were appointed at St. Peter's to help Adam Raby solicit subscriptions to buy a house suitable for services in the Kimberton area. The committee decided on the old Friends Meeting House built in 1822 by Emmor Kimber. The owners were Joseph Tyson, Eli Huzzard and John Rees. A purchase price was set of $1,700 with John Rees very charitably selling his share for $50 as long as the property was used for church purposes. On January 4, 1874, after a service conducted by the Reverend Peter Raby, the congregation of St. Peter's agreed to the purchase and agreed to meet the price by buying subscriptions from the church. The deed to the property was turned over to St. Peter's on April 2, 1874 after most of the price was met. At this time, informal meetings must have been held as two men were appointed to take up collections at the Kimberton Chapel. A reference in the Village Record of February 7, 1874 reads "Kimberton Meeting House."

On March 20, 1876, the Rev. J. Frank Hartman continued to supervise the work on the new church building and was generally regarded and listed as the official organizer of Centennial Lutheran Church. At this time $41 was collected for fitting the building as a place of worship. Sometime during the week of October 4, 1876, the church was officially dedicated and named the Centennial Evangelical Lutheran Church, as the Centennial Exhibition was underway in Philadelphia at the time.

Original Centennial Evangelical Lutheran Church members are:

Barber, Emma and Sallie
Bartlett, Maggie
Beaver, Eliza and Jacob
Bush, Henrietta, Elmer and Mary Ann
Detterline, George
Dimm, Mary, Maggie Charles
Detwiler, Mary, Ella, Hannah, and Catherine
Dimm, Evangeline, Martha
Christman, Charles Ecklhardt, Emma Evans, Maggie, Darlington
Emery, William, Sarah
Francis, Mary Harple, Jesse Hippie, Joan Holman, John
Kauler, Daniel, Mary, D. Web
Keely, Morgan Lightcap, Lillie King, Mary Esther
March, Benjamin, Sarah, Annie, L.P.
Miller, Emma, Florence, Anna May
Peterson, Bernard
Pennypacker, Ruthie
Piersol, Eliza
Raby, P.P., Lizzie, Peter, Ed I. and David Rambo, Kate
Root, Isaac, Hannah, John and David
Moore, Amelia Shaffer, George
Thomas, David, Harriet, Lillie
Wadsworth, Thomas, Mrs. Thomas
Wagner, Annie
Walton, Abel, Josephine
Wilson, Mrs. L.A., Samaria, Ida, Mary and Ellie
Snyder, William,
Pugh, Emma

Kimber Family Cemetery

A deed was granted to the Emmor Kimber Family Cemetery. On January 14, 1897, Martha Kimber conveyed the cemetery to Centennial Lutheran Church for $1. Martha had inherited from her sister the remainder of the Kimber estate. The cemetery remained under the care of the church. The remains of Emmor Kimber, Susanne, Samuel, Susanna (another daughter), Gertrude, Henrietta Deville, Benjamin March, Livingston March, and others were buried there.

Kimber Family Cemetery at Kimberton Centennial Evangelical Lutheran Church grounds.

Kimber Cemetery individual grave stone.

Kimberton Grange

A group of 46 neighborhood men joined together on November 14, 1885 and formed the Washington Camp No. 93 of Pennsylvania of the Patriotic Order of the Sons of America. In 1888, they purchased two lots from the Dutton Madden subdivision and built the present building. They held the property for a short time, selling it to William R. Snyder in 1892. Snyder, Root & Co. operated a planing mill, machine shop and foundry in the building. It was probably by this company that the building was enlarged in the back. The company made window frames, door jambs and sash as well as the products of the machine shop and foundry. It operated as such until 1910 when it was purchased by John Gyger, one of the Trustees of the Kimberton Grange.

Kimberton Grange #1304 Meeting Place. Kimberton Pa.

The Kimberton Grange #1304 was situated in the village of Kimberton and is an active part of this community today. Through the efforts of John and Daniel Gyger, a meeting was called for February 8, 1906 for the purpose of organizing a Grange. It was a bad winter night with rain and fog. As this was in the horse and buggy days, it was not a fit night for horses to stand out in the weather, so the crowd was small. There were 41 persons who braved the elements and signed up as charter members. Mr. George North and a Mr. Moore from Lyndell Grange, two men dedicated to the work of the order, showed great courage in driving over muddy roads on such a night to assist in organizing this Grange. Officers were selected and installed by Mr. North, doing the work entirely by memory, making the ceremony a very impressive one.

The first Master was John Gyger, the first lecturer, Daniel Gyger and the first secretary, Katie Funk Yeager. It was a very humble beginning, meetings being held in the second floor of the building.

Kimberton Grange hamburger stand at the Kimberton Fair.

The room at that time was used for the high school. The lower floor was a planing mill. It was necessary to borrow some oil lamps from Allison Yeager, who owned the store across the way as there was no electricity in Kimberton at that time. Meetings were continued to be held in this room with rent being paid of $3.00 per month and $.50 per meeting janitor fee.

Yeager's Store (Montgomery Bodick Store).

High School

There are only four known schools to have existed within the bounds of the Kimberton Historic District, the first being Emmor Kimber's French Creek Boarding School for Girls. This building was built to be a public high school and to replace the high school that had been held in the Patriotic Order of the Sons of America (P.O.S.) hall ever since 1899. In 1906, there were 38 pupils from 4 one-room schools in the township. The building was finished in 1907 and was used as a high school for only a few years, when it was converted into a grade school for the village. Yet, there were not enough pupils. Those who wanted a high school education were sent to Phoenixville. As a grade school, this building operated until 1928, when a multi-roomed consolidated school was built at the northeastern end of the village.

Kimberton High School

About 1925, Frank Foster, a retired businessman, purchased several farm properties in the three townships; Charlestown, Schuylkill, and East Pikeland. He felt that one - room schools were inadequate and urged the taxpayers to build a consolidated school, for which he offered to pay half the cost. Construction costs were low at that time. There was a law at the time which limited the School Boards to the amount of money which they could spend without the consent of the majority of the taxpayers, therefore, it had to be decided by a popular vote at the general election. The first time it was voted down. However, the second election, after much canvassing by the supporters of the project, they approved the idea and it carried with a fair majority. Mr. Foster made good his promise and presented the School Board a check for $47,000. The school was dedicated on October 16, 1938.

Pickering Valley Railroad

The village remained quiet until railroad fever struck. The Pickering Valley Line was built in 1871 from Phoenixville to Byers (Eagle). It was both a passenger and a freight line, carrying iron ore to Phoenix Iron Works, and milk and farm products to the Reading Railroad depot in Phoenixville for shipment to Philadelphia. Kimberton station was the finest on the line and was a manned station unlike others which were "flag" stations where the trains stopped only on request. Sidings were built to serve a coaling business and feed warehouse, and to allow the passing of trains. A cattle auction was set up within close proximity of the station, since cattle and horses were brought in by train.

Kimberton Train Station circa 1908

The center of the village moved to the east side of the town. A new general store, creameries, foundries, planing mills, Patriotic Sons of America Hall and the Grange Hall were established. In 1915, an electrical short circuit on the telephone wires set the wooden train station ablaze. The station was replaced with stone and brick, the only remaining station on the line today.

Kimberton Train Station today

As Kimberton became the largest milk shipping station on the Pickering Valley Line, a building used to receive and cool the milk prior to shipping it on to Phoenixville and Philadelphia, was first used by Supplee - Alderney, then Supplee, Wills, Jones Company, then Harbison Dairies, then Gross' Dairies. All of these companies were based in Philadelphia.

The Old Milk Station Supplee's Alderney Dairy in Kimberton.

As truck shipping began to cut into the railroad business, it was eventually sold for warehouse space to Roberts Packing Company.

A train wreck occurred on October 4, 1877, one mile East of Kimberton. Rain-swollen creeks with no culvert washed the railroad tracks out. The engine, running backward killed 8 people. Two Kimberton residents, William and Sadie Hallman, were killed in the train wreck. Settlement from the railroad was $400.

Kimberton Blacksmith Shop

The Kimberton Blacksmith Shop, located next to the Kimberton Country House, is a very significant part of the Kimberton Historic District. It was a very necessary adjunct to the early village and mill, as well as to the settlers in building their homesteads. That it has remained almost unchanged for possibly two hundred years is commendable. This small piece of Kimberton has been commercially used in various ways since inception of the village. It was sold with a dwelling house, blacksmith shop and 45 acres of land in 1944 to George Moses. The store became a bakery in 1887, operated by Augustus Malenke, and into the 1930s as the Schultz Baking Company which delivered door-to-door. It was sold then to Herford Wells, who operated a grocery and gas station there while the small barn was leased to the first Kimberton Fire Company in 1929. The Fire Company was organized under the leadership of John Kasitz. The house and store burned on June 6, 1936, when Mrs. Wells' apron, saturated with gasoline fumes, caught fire in her kitchen and, in casting it off, the building was ignited. For lack of keys to the fire truck, the truck was rolled out by hand, but the building was lost, The Wells rebuilt and continued their grocery and gas station business. In recent years, the store has been used as a crystals and stone gift shop.

Kimberton Blacksmith Shop which became the Kimberton Fire Station.

Wayne Emory, who owned and operated the bakery after Mr. Schultz, was among the first to own an automobile. It was a five passenger Maxwell which he enjoyed driving for the pleasure of his family and friends. They had three daughters, one not yet of school age.

Five Seater Maxwell Automobile

During the autumn months of 1905 or 1906 they decided to drive to Pottstown on a shopping tour of the town. They invited Mr. Emery's sister and brother-in-law, Jacob and Sally Reese, along with them. The women wore broad-brimmed hats tied down with a scarf and tan dusters. The driver also wore a duster, plus large leather gauntlets, cap and goggles. This may seem strange today, but the early autos doors to get into the front seat, were not standard equipment. Neither were windshields nor headlights. Their driving was done during daylight hours.

They entered Pottstown at Keim Street, over the Pennsylvania Railroad grade crossing without incident, but a few yards further the Reading Company had a grade crossing with a sharp incline up to the tracks. It has never been determined whether their view of the oncoming train was obstructed or if they were not alert to the danger, but they proceeded onto the tracks where their new car was completely demolished and four of the occupants were killed by the impact of the fast-moving passenger train. Mr. Emery survived with injuries that kept him hospitalized for several months, but he made a complete recovery. The funeral procession of those lost in the wreck proceeded with four horse-drawn hearses up the dusty road to Pikeland Cemetery and was a sad and unforgettable scene to all who witnessed it.

Kimberton Fair

The first Kimberton Fair was held in 1929 at the farm of Henry Supiot. In the mid-1930s, the fair moved to another Supiot field at the east end of the farm (Maple Lawn). In August, 1936, the Kimberton Fire Company purchased 17 acres at the present site. The first apparatus room for the Kimberton Fire Company was built in 1950 at this site. The Kimberton Fair has been held at this site every year except for several years during World War II.

Kimberton Community Fair 1987 [6]

Other Kimberton Businesses

A.C. Roberts began a meat packing enterprise in Kimberton in 1918. This business was active until the mid-1970s.

A.C. Roberts Packing Company, Kimberton PA.

Kimberton Roberts Water Tower torn down Dec 23, 1996

Napkin from Roberts Meat Packing Company, Kimberton Pa.

Frank Detwiler and Sons, next to the Kimberton Market, have produced veteran's grave markers and flag emblems at this location since 1921.

Detwiler Machine Shop

Dutton Madden, a developer, built all of the brick houses in Kimberton in the late 1880s.

Carl Miller, another developer, built stone homes in the Valley Dell area in 1940 for approximately $3950 each.

Soon after moving from Huntington County to Kimberton in 1922, J. Mell Kimmel laid out 40 building lots on the road between Phoenixville and Kimberton called Kimberton Heights (near the Fire House).

Dr. Robert Griffith was the local physician who carried on a family tradition of caring for the ills, births and deaths of the area known as Kimberton. For 101 years, the Griffith doctors, Joseph and his son, Robert, practiced medicine in the village. Dr. Joseph Griffith, a graduate of the University of Pennsylvania, lived at the Boarding School Inn from about 1829 until 1833 when he moved to a house on Hares Hill Road. He remained on Hares Hill Road seven years when he moved to a farm just outside of the village, west, on Kimberton Road. Son Robert, was born on that property in 1845, married in 1878, and purchased the three continuous lots of Dutton Madden's plan in 1884 and built the house in 1888.

C.S. Wilson and Sons

Jugan Barber Shop in Kimberton.

Chapter 2. West on Seven Stars

These are the stories, places and people who lived near West Seven Stars Road in East Vincent Township, Chester County, Pennsylvania.

West Seven Stars Road [7]

Pikeland Iron Works

Starting on East Pikeland boundary line going down the hill you hardly notice a culvert and race-way. On the left side you observe a waterway. This water race was to divert water from the French Creek to turn a water wheel for power.

Mill race way.

Today, there is a depression in the ground where the water was once diverted.

Mill race depression

A German steel maker by the name of Clement Roentgen built a small forge on the bank called "Pikeland Iron Works". Heating pig iron and pounding out the impurities with a large hammer to make iron workable. He made iron bars for the navy around the time 1813. The water wheel was to power his big trip hammer. He would fix wagon wheels for personal transportation (buggy's) and wheels for hauling products. Roentgen was put out of business because of a patent problem.

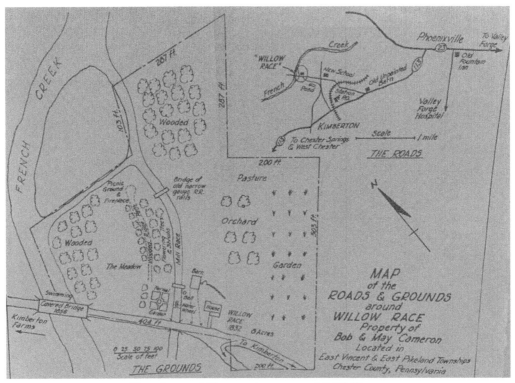

Roads and Grounds around Mill Race

On the same plot, the Witmers Atlas of 1873 records Edward Miller Machine shop and saw mill was there.

Typical Machine Shop Advertisement:

Miller is a millwright and machinist. Manufactures the most improved threshing machine in the best style and repairs every type of agriculture implements (tools). - Kimberton PA

Next on location is John Eckhart, who had a wheel shop around 1890. Sometime later, the business property was used as a summer house.

Former wheel shop location, summer house as it is today.

Movie Filming Location: Phoenixville and Kimberton

In 1952, a motion picture was made at the Valley Forge General Hospital in Phoenixville. A story about a young man blinded in the war, then having his sight restored and discovered his best friend was African American.

One scene was shot on the porch of the (summer) house and the other one fishing in the French Creek. The film was called *"Bright Victory"*.

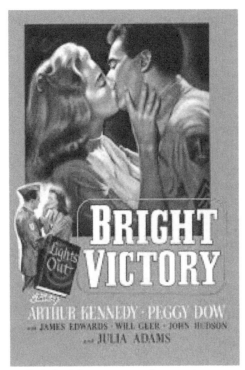

Bright Victory movie poster.
Movie filmed near Kennedy Covered Bridge.

Kennedy Covered Bridge

As the population increased, farm products sales increased. It was important to have a bridge that crossed the French Creek especially in winter weather. It was Alexander Kennedy's influence that the county commissioners approved the petition to construct the bridge.

Kennedy Bridge, about a mile upstream near the Kimberton Waldorf School, was built in 1856. This bridge was built at the site of Kennedy's Ford on the French Creek. The bridge is located on West Seven Stars Road.

This 100 foot bridge carries the inscription: "Built for Newton Nichols, Albert Way and Wm.G. Maitland, county commissioners. Built by Jesse King and and Alex King in 1856.

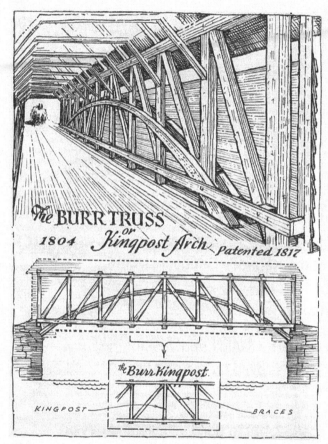

Burr Truss

Theodore Burr (1771-1822) A native of Connecticut, Burr studied bridge building in his youth, and in 1804 patented the famous Burr Arch Truss. This curved arch design was used in the famous Camelback bridge at Harrisburg and on many of the early Pennsylvania bridges.

The three local bridges crossing the French Creek are all of this design.

The Pennsylvania Covered Bridge Society is named for Theodore Burr.

Kennedy Bridge is a Burr Truss design.

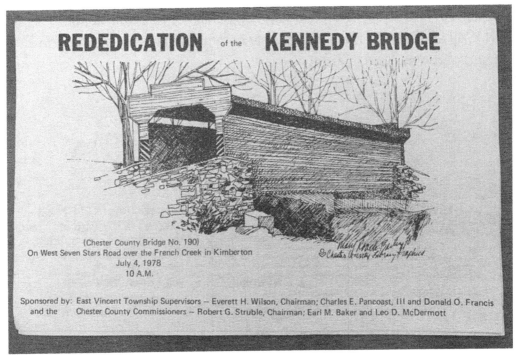

Rededication of the Kennedy Bridge in 1978.[8]

Additional details on the Kennedy Bridge:

> "Built in 1856 by Alex Kennedy & Alex and Jesse King ...
> Rehabilitated in 1978 ... Destroyed by fire on May 10, 1986 ...
> Rehabilitated in 1987"

The Chester County bridge cost $2,149 to build initially and has an unusual portal design. The bridge was destroyed by an arsonist in 1986.

Smoldering fire Kennedy Bridge 1986

Firefighters inspecting the bridge remains.

After the fire, a band of concerned citizens was formed to circulate a petition to rebuild the bridge. I was chairman of that committee. By September we had the Theodore Burr Covered Bridge Society of Pennsylvania collect almost 5,000 signatures to petition the county commissioners to rebuild the covered bridge. See Appendix: Kennedy Covered Bridge Fire and Restoration for newspaper accounts.

Temporary Kennedy Bridge used for
several years until new bridge was built.

Constructing new Kennedy Bridge

Kennedy Bridge on West Seven Stars Road, Kimberton PA

Before presenting the petitions to the commissioners, we received word they were going to replace the bridge. The bridge was built with bongossi wood from Africa and would not burn. Prefab in York County and assembled on site it was dedicated the next year. The bridge is owned and maintained by Chester County, Pennsylvania.

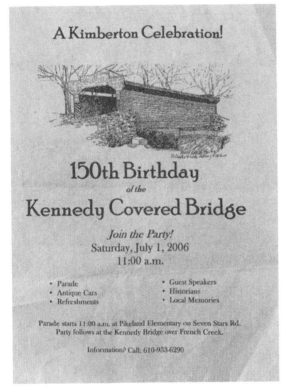

Kennedy Covered Bridge 150th Anniversary posters.

150th Birthday Celebration of the Kennedy Covered Bridge.

Vintage cars procession on 150th Anniversary in 2006.[9]

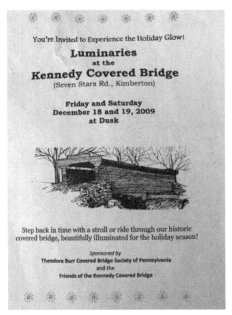

Friends of the Kennedy Covered Bridge luminaries announcement.

Luminaries at the Kennedy Covered Bridge. Christmas holiday 2019.

Pennsylvania Capital Scandal

The State Capitol in Harrisburg had a disastrous fire in 1897 and the capitol was lost. Four million dollars was approved to rebuild the Capitol.

Fire at the Capitol, Harrisburg, Pennsylvania

The architect Joseph M. Huston, auditor General William Snyder and State Treasurer were appointed to the commission. Before the capitol was finished another three million dollars was added to complete the building. That October, U.S. President Theodore Roosevelt dedicated the building. Everyone was pleased about the new building and the low cost.

STATE CAPITOL, HARRISBURG, PA.

The New Capitol Building

The state celebrated the new capitol, but it did not last long. A new administration began their term in January and William H. Berry became the new treasurer. He discovered and announced that the Capitol had actually cost 13 million dollars.

Berry became suspicious when he discovered a workman's bill that the person could not have done that much work in that short a period of time. Ceiling costs were estimated at $550 and billed for $5,500. Contractor John Sanderson supplied a chandelier and billed $183,500 and other bills for furniture. Berry estimated the new capital cost five million dollars more than budgeted.

The new governor, John H. Fischer appointed a commission to investigate.

The state obtained a conviction against architect Huston, contractor Sanderson and auditor Snyder. The defendants delayed sentencing by appeals. After much finger pointing the state dropped the case. Snyder continued to live in East Vincent until his death. He is buried in a mausoleum at East Vincent United Church of Christ on Route 23 in East Vincent Township. [10]

Kennedy Farm - Origins

Alexander Kennedy was the third son of the Kennedy clan in the lime business in Port Kennedy, Pennsylvania next to Valley Forge Park. There were approximately 400 people working in this lime business.

In the 1850s he moved to East Vincent Township on West Seven Stars Road. He was listed as a farmer and extensive dealer in livestock and president of the bank of Phoenixville. He built an elegant stone house. The family was known for their grand parties and casual event. The bridge crossing the French Creek was named for him.

Kennedy House at The Kimberton Waldorf School.[11]

Honorable William P. Snyder

William P. Snyder was a former member of the Pennsylvania House of Representatives, a senator and a Auditor General. Retiring in 1906 Snyder bought 400 acres in East Vincent Township on West Seven Stars Road from Alex Kennedy. Snyder remodeled the house and built a conservatory with a glass dome in the middle of the house, filled with tropical plants, a porch, balcony and large columns in front. The house remains today with a stone wall along West Seven Stars Road. His stable was full of show horses and basset hound dogs. He also had an extensive collection of firearms. Snyder employed a number of local helpers and collected expensive automobiles. Truly a man of wealth.

Kimberton Farms School

Mr. H.A.W. Myrin, a Norwegian oil man and his wife Mable Pew Myrin (daughter of Sun Oil founder, Joseph "Newton" Pew (1848 – 1912)) were looking for acreage in the area. Their daughter was a student at Bryn Mawr College. They bought the Snyder property and two others as well as three farms in West Vincent Township. This was in 1940.

WWII planes in action.

The school was originally designed to care for British children. London, England at the time was under siege by German warplanes. The London Home Office decided not to let children travel because of the fear of the German submarines attacking the ships crossing the Atlantic.

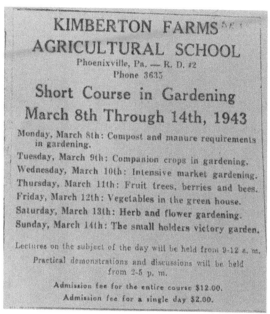

Kimberton Farms School gardening course advertisement.

Kimberton Farms had been chosen as a demonstration center for biodynamic method of farming and gardening. Biodynamic farming is a form of alternative agriculture very similar to organic farming. The purpose of this method is to combine soil conservation without the use of fertilizer or chemicals. [12]

Kimberton Farms field across the road from Kimberton Waldorf School.

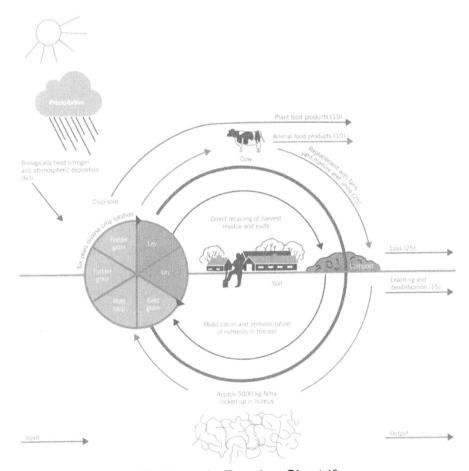

Biodynamic Farming Chart [13]

The management of the farm was supervised by Dr. Ehrenfried Pfeiffer. A vegetable garden and greenhouse were situated near the main building. Facilities include rooms for the students, lecture rooms, a library and a living room. Not only is the demonstration of soil conservation through for example, cover crops (winter planting to enrich soil in the summer), but also the proper way of using manure compost.

The south farm on West Seven Stars Road pasture was valuable land for a herd of Aberdeen Angus beef cattle.

Aberdeen Angus Beef Cattle[14]

The East Farm on Miller Road is a dairy herd consisting of registered Guernsey and Holstein cows. The pupils are trained in all routine planting of farm crops, plowing, harrowing, manure and compost treatment. Feeding and maintaining the livestock became the foundation of the farm practice.

Alarik Myrin (1884-1970) and Mabel Pew Myrin (1889-1972)

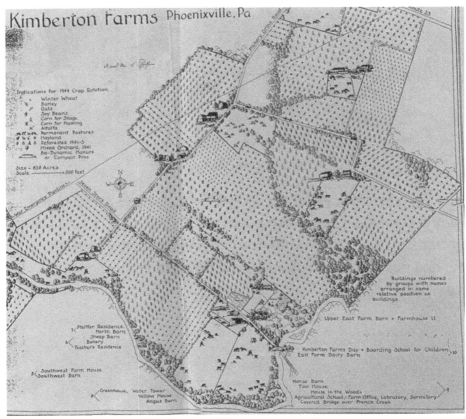

Kimberton Farms property.

This practice of agriculture is based on the teaching of a popular Austrian thinker, Rudolf Steiner. Steiners practice of agriculture teaching attracted the attention of Alarik and Mabel Myrin.

Rudolf Steiner (1861-1925) in 1919

"The heart of the Waldorf method is the conviction that education is an art – it must speak to the child's experience. To educate the whole child, the heart must be reached, as well as the mind."
— Rudolf Steiner, founder of Waldorf education

As teachers of the Farm School worked, they needed a day care center for the children of employees and started one on Miller Road. When the agriculture business closed, pupils were moved to the Kennedy Mansion on Seven Stars Road. Each year a grade was added until it became a K-12 school known as Kimberton Waldorf School.

A biodynamic farm. Chopping corn while the sun comes up on Seven Stars Road.[15]

Kimberton Waldorf School

The Kimberton Farms School name was changed to Kimberton Waldorf School around 1985.

Rudolf Steiner was a key influencer of The Kimberton Waldorf School. Not only was he instrumental in the biodynamic farming methods, but he also was a reformer of the education system of the time.

Kimberton Waldorf School on West Seven Stars Road. [16]

I look into the world
And see the shining sun;
I see the sparkling stars;
I see the quiet stones;
The plants have a life and grow;
The beasts in feeling live;
A dwelling in their souls
Men to the spirit give.

I look into the world
That lives within myself.

God's Spirit lives and weaves
In light of sun and soul,
In heights of world without,
In depths of soul within.

To thee of spirit of God,
In praying do I turn,
That strength and grace and skill
For learning and for work
In me may live and grow. [17]

Rudolf Steiner

Kimberton Waldorf School

Kimberton Waldorf School from West Seven Stars Road

Seven Stars Yogurt Farm

The Kimberton Waldorf School separated itself from the farm operation and subsequently leased the farm to Seven Starts Yogurt Farm, which remains in operation today as a yogurt producing farm.

Jersey cows at Seven Stars Yogurt Farm, with Kimberton Farms origins.[18]

An explanation of a biodynamic farm:

> "We supplement this foundation of organics with the biodynamic perspective of looking at the farm as a living organism. Based on the teachings and spiritual insight of Austrian philosopher Rudolph Steiner, biodynamics recognizes the interconnected relationship of the soil, plants, animals, and the cosmos. With the goal of creating a self-sustaining and ecologically balanced farm, we replenish the soil through crop diversification and rotation; and we revitalize the soil's nutrients by herbal preparations and farm composts." [19]
> - Seven Stars Yogurt Farm

Seven Stars Yogurt Farm, Kimberton PA on West Seven Stars Road. [20]

Biodynamic farmers manage their farms as a diversified, self-contained, self-sustaining organism. According to the Biodynamic Association, "It is the biodiversity of the farm, organized so that the waste of one part of the farm becomes the energy for another, that results in an increase in the farm's capacity for self-renewal and ultimately makes the farm sustainable." [21]

"Biodynamic farms don't use GMOs, synthetic chemicals, fertilizers, or pesticides. Instead, they rely on methods such as compost, green manures, cover crops, and companion plants."
- Kimberton Whole Foods

Cow enjoying life at Seven Stars Yogurt Farm. [22]

Cows roaming in field owned by Seven Stars Yogurt Farm.

Kimberton Community Supported Agriculture (CSA)

"Kimberton CSA is a ten acre biodynamic, organic mixed vegetable farm. The first CSA in Pennsylvania, this farm was started in 1987 by the Kimberton Waldorf School and interested members of the community looking for ways of doing business that would best support the local community, local agriculture and provide for the needs of everyone involved, including those of our environment."

- Kimberton CSA

Kimberton CSA on West Seven Stars Road. [23]

Rainbow over the Kimberton CSA [24]

Rogers / Beaver Farm

"The nearest neighbor after crossing the boundaries of Phoenixville were
a family by the name of Rogers, living in a cave on the French Creek
seven miles distant. The time was 1712 to 1714." [25]

- Samuel Pennypacker

Beaver Farm House

It was the perfect spot for Joseph Rogers, "The Settler" to establish a homestead. An Indian village below the barn had cleared the land of trees for firewood and there were some open spaces to plant a crop. A large overhang or cave was perfect spot to build a temporary house. First "Joseph the Settler" then "Joseph the Younger" established a family on the farm. In 1838 the family moved to Pendleton, Indiana. The farm was subdivided to Henry Hoffman. The main farm later sold to Daniel Beaver in 1863.

Daniel, Jacob and Frank Beaver were all prosperous and successful farmers. Frank Beaver's son did not want to be a farmer. Upon graduation from West Chester Normal School (later became West Chester University). Beaver got a job teaching Electrical Engineering at Lehigh University in Bethlehem PA. He taught and lived there for 47 years. He also received a degree from MIT. Dr. Beaver inherited the Beaver Farm and this became his summer home on Seven Stars Road.

Left: Beaver Farm House before electric.
Right: Beaver Farm today

A new tenant house was built near the barn for a farmer in 1929. The old homestead was remodeled with a modern heating system, electric, plumbing in addition to a swimming pool and tennis court. Dr. Beaver retired here in 1964 and passed away in 1975. His daughter Ann lived in the house until 2002 when she sold the property to CampHill.

Beaver farm barn then (left in 1952) and now (right in 2019).

The Camphill Special School is private boarding and day school for children with intellectual and developmental disabilities. It is an accredited Waldorf school, celebrating its 100th anniversary in 2019.

Beaver Farm at Camphill Special School

Walter and Clyde Scheib

It was a good year on March 1, 1929. My father mother, sister and I (Clyde Scheib) moved to the J.L. Beaver Farm.

Walter Scheib, authors father.

The house was two years old and had electric service. With electricity we could run an electric milking machine for cows allowing us to increase our herd to thirty cows. Two years later a farm silo was built, water installed and a bathroom in the house. In 1940 the barn was remodeled to metal stalls. This was our well kept fenced-in farm.

Wall Street Crash of 1929

At the end of 1929, the stock market crashed. After one year cash and money dried up. Banks closed with your money. Factories and stores also closed. Home and farm mortgages were foreclosed. Many people were out of work. You did not have any money to survive. Food, grain, market meat prices dropped but we managed to eat from the farm products.

My fathers dairy stopped picking up milk because the customers could not pay. People moved in with other relatives and did anything to make a dime.

Growing Up in the Depression
The 1930s

As a small child I don't remember much about the hard times. I lived on a farm and we grew much of our food with a garden, pigs and beef. You only bought the necessities at the store; sugar, salt, coffee, tea, etc. The

American store did not sell meat, fish or fresh fruit since there was no refrigeration.

Hucksters would come along the road with fish and fresh fruit.

The family would venture on Saturday night to Phoenixville, the closest major town, to shop.

Much of your life was centered around the kitchen stove. It also heated the whole house in the winter. The farm kept my father and hired man busy taking care of the animals. We always had a hired man. My mother kept busy feeding and clothing us, a full time job.

Amos "n" Andy was a popular radio program in the 1920s and 30s.

We finally bought a radio to play music. We kids listened to the Tom Mix, Orphan Annie, Jack Armstrong. As a family we listened to Amos n' Andy, Lowell Thomas and Jack Benny.

Tom Mix popular on radio and film late 1920s

There was a hand pump for water on the back porch. When you wanted water, you hand cranked the handle. An outdoor bench had basins, soap, and towels. When coming in from the field you drew the water and mixed with warm water you washed your hands and face before entering the house.

My father took the milk to the Kimberton receiving station in an old coupe car with a box in the rumble seat. Our lifestyle was simple.

Rumble seat in 1928 Hudson

The 1940s

Factories began to reopen and men found work. The war in Europe was starting and in 1941 the USA declared war on Germany and Japan. Younger men were drafted. I was not drafted since I was needed to farm.

Store inventory was sold but could not be replaced because of the war emergency. Auto production stopped, so there were no new cars.

Gas rationing, shoe rationing, tires, meat and sugar rationed as well. No pleasure driving was allowed except church outings. Some air raid drills were conducted resulting in planned blackout of houses and business.

The hired man got drafted and my father and a 14 year old boy (me) ran the farm. When I was 18 years old near the end of the war, I got a agriculture deferment to produce food. As WWII ended, production of farm machinery began with new modern tractors that could do the work of many.

1943 Farmall Tractor (International Harvester)

These machines improved the planting and harvesting and hand labor.

I married Alda Wenger in 1948 and we lived in an apartment in the farm house. In 1954 the farm owner gave us a 1/2 acre to build a new house on 7 Stars Road and Hickory Grove Road. We raised four children with three of them graduating from Delaware Valley University. Although I did not receive a large salary, we always had new cars, house furnishings and modern appliances.

Author Clyde and wife Alda circa 1948

In the 1960s we had increased our dairy herd to almost 90 head and 1,000 laying hens (100 dozen eggs per week) on two farms. We connected with Penn State Extension Service (county agents) and the children joined the 4H Club Program.

Authors cows crossing West Seven Star Road, Kimberton PA

We started to raise registered Guernsey dairy cattle over the years we had a show cow string of prized cattle. We attended eight shows a year. The county agents had dairy meetings in the winter months to teach you to improve production and improve the sanitary conditions on the farm.

Tenant house (1952) side view on West Seven Stars Road.
Author's family lived in tenant house.

After my father, Walter Scheib passed away in December 1985, I downsized the farm. In 1995 I had a terrible accident in a fall in the barn and stopped milking cows. I cropped farm until it was sold in 2001.

Tenant house today from West Seven Stars Road.

Author's home on West Seven Stars Road.

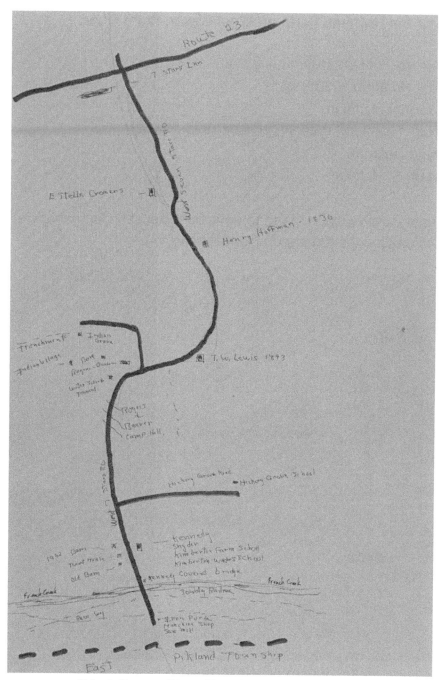

West Seven Stars Road sketch by author.

Owners of the Hoffman Farm on West Seven Stars Road

The past owners of the Hoffman farm are:
- Henry Hoffman 1830
- Alexander Hoffman
- William Hoffman - road supervisor 1928-1932
- Wayne Hoffman
- William S. Hoffman

The Hoffman family sold the farm to developer Benson Companies in 2001, who created the Kimberton Hunt subdivision.

Hoffman barn on West Seven Stars Road.

Kimberton Hunt Subdivision formerly Hoffman Farm. Heritage Drive (shown) connects to West Seven Stars Road.

Kimberton Hunt subdivision entrance on old Hoffman Farm.

Estelle Harrop Cremers (1925-2010)

The next farm on the left side of West Seven Stars Road is the William Cremers Sr. farm. Estelle Cremers is the daughter-in-law of William Sr. and wife of William Jr.

Estelle was an accomplished soloist at Valley Forge Memorial Chapel. When her singing career ended, Estelle began historical research, searching land records as part of the French and Pickering Conservation Land Trust. She lived on West Seven Stars Road for 17 years.

Estelle Cremers circa 1986 [26]

Mrs. Cremers prepared numerous properties for the National Register of Historical places in her work for the land trust.

Cremers house off West Seven Stars Road.

She wrote; the History of Warwick Township; *30,000 Acres, Vincent and Pikeland Townships 1686 to 1850; Reading Furnace 1736;* and writings for the three Coventry townships. Estelle passed away on November 28, 2010, and is sadly missed by her friends.

Estelle Cremer's landmark 1989 book.

Seven Stars Inn

Seven Stars Inn is located on West Seven Stars Road and Route 23 in East Vincent Township. Let us clear up the confusion of Gerhard Brumbach and the Seven Stars Inn. Although one-half of the Brumbach Tavern dates from 1736, the Seven Stars Inn actually dates from 1754. The Seven Stars Inn is incorrectly known as being from 1736.

Brumbach Tavern had a different class of patrons and was more like a hotel while The Seven Stars Inn was like a motel.

Drovers with herds of cattle on the way to market let the cattle graze in the field while the Drovers slept wherever they could, in the Seven Stars Inn. Cattle and horse sales were held in the barn and fox hunting was done in the nearby fields on occasion.

Seven Stars Inn historical sketch.[27]

The Seven Stars Inn has in the past been the voting place in the East Vincent Township and a meeting place for the supervisor's meetings.

Seven Stars Inn advertisement (1957)

The Seven Stars Inn was closed during prohibition and became a working farm. Russell Latshaw opened an ice cream bar in 1940 at the inn. Over the years the restaurant changed hands and is in operation today as the Seven Stars Inn.

Historic Seven Stars Inn today.

The end of the road.

Chapter 3. Parker Ford Village

Many years ago my neighbor and historian Estelle Cremers gave me the background of Parker's Tavern in Parker Ford and its place in history. She said, "save that building, restore and maintain it".

I therefore got involved in efforts to preserve and protect Parker's Tavern as Chairman of the East Vincent Township Historical Commission. As such I have collected the details and culture around the tavern, the canal and the Parker Ford Village in general.

Over the years, we conducted historical walking tours of Parker Ford Village or Olde Parkerford as it was also known. It was one of East Vincent Township's historical villages of Chester County, Pennsylvania. The tours included remnants of the Girard Canal in Parker Ford, Parker's Tavern, a mule barn and several historic houses and farms.

Historic Parker's Tavern

Parker's Tavern is located in the village known as Parker Ford, a National Historic District (1982). The Parker Ford District was deemed historically significant in the areas of commerce, transportation and military history between the years 1700 - 1899. General Washington's Continental troops crossed the Schuylkill River adjacent to the village, in September of 1777, after the Battle of Brandywine.

Parker's Tavern [28]

The Tavern was built in 1766 by Edward Parker. His son, Henry, built the home which has been restored and that stands today across from the Tavern and is known formally as The Henry Parker House but also informally as Ann Tudor's House, the last resident to live on the property.

Foreground is canal and back of Henry Parker House.
Parker's Tavern in background.

The village was located along what was once known as the "Great Road" from Philadelphia to Reading. Like other taverns that dotted the landscape, it provided an important respite for weary travelers, along with serving as a center of commerce and entertainment for the community. Parker's Tavern remained in use to serve travelers that made their way on the newly opened Schuylkill River Canal, a system of man-made waterways that connected Philadelphia with the coal regions of the northern counties. Throughout most of the nineteenth century, the Parker Ford village remained an active center of transportation and commerce.[29]

Parker Ford Village

The Parker Ford village consists of a tavern, stable building & three houses built during the mid-18th century. These early buildings stand on both sides of the early river trail which caught traffic from the ford and from the west bank of the Schuylkill River.

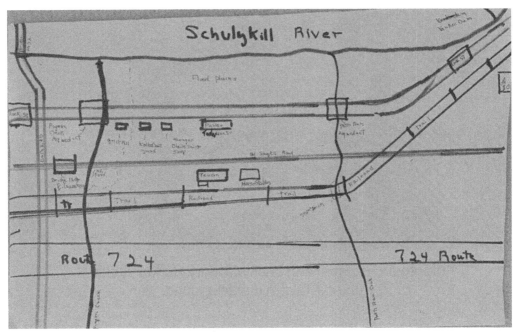

Parker Ford Village landmarks sketch by author. (2019)

The buildings are well-preserved and relatively unchanged since there have been few renovations through the years.

84

Parkers House (Ann Tudors House).

Back of Parkers House with steps to canal.

Next to house was Favinger Blacksmith Shop, Kolbs Boat Yard and a Grist Mill.

Washington's Crossing

In September 1777, General Washington and his men, on their "race for the fords," crossed the Schuylkill River at Parker Ford, Pennsylvania. Though it was one of the more shallow fords on the river, heavy rainfall delayed the crossing. While he waited for the river to recede, Washington passed through Parker Ford and may have stopped near Parker's Tavern.

Scene Outside a Tavern [30]

After the Revolution the village remained an integral part of the transportation system in the state. The tavern continued to serve travelers and provide a source of commerce for local residents.

It's Place in History

In 1768, Edward Parker built a fine tavern at the Schuylkill ford known thereafter as Parker Ford. Edward Parker had been a tavern keeper in Coventry Township at least as early as 1748. The Vincent location at the natural place of crossing was a much better business spot and this tavern became one of the best in the area. Just within the bounds of Vincent Township, where Pigeon Creek enters the Schuylkill River, a grist mill was built in 1740. Several tradesmen's shops were built nearby: a blacksmith shop, a boatyard and stables. [31]

A great change came to this little village at Parker's Tavern when the Schuylkill Valley branch of the Pennsylvania Railroad (PRR) located their tracks one quarter of a mile west of the ford in East Coventry Township. A passenger and freight station was built and named Lawrenceville. Due to a conflict of names, the station and village were renamed Parker Ford.

PRR Train going through Parker Ford

Revolutionary War

Many of the colonists who came to the New World placed their left hands on the Bible and with raised right hand pledged allegiance to the King of England, King Charles II (1630–1685), and the British Empire, a pledge that was not to be taken lightly. To strike against the crown was a traitor's act. Not all of the citizens were for the rebellion.

In July 1777, General William Howe changed plans to invade Philadelphia by way of Trenton, New Jersey. News of the embarkation of a large British force at New York suggested the idea that the attack on the capital of Pennsylvania would be by way of the Delaware River. So sure that the enemy expected to capture Philadelphia, General Washington was ordered to march to the vicinity of the city.

General Howe's fleet was sighted August 8 at the Chesapeake Bay. Finding the Delaware River more difficult to navigate than he had expected, he made his approach by the way of the Chesapeake Bay.

The fleet passed up the Elk River as far as the ships could be navigated with safety. On the 25th of August, he landed 18,000 men with supplies and all the implements of war. General Washington's army passed through Philadelphia and took position near Chadd's Ford on the Brandywine Creek in Chester County. It was a natural place for General Washington to set up a defense. War had come to Chester County.

Washington directing his troops at Battle of Brandywine.[32]

The column of British troops under General Cornwallis' command entered Chester County on the 11th of September. The British army divided into two columns: one to continue to Chadd's Ford, the other to the north to the high grounds of Birmingham Meeting House. General Sullivan who commanded the right wing of the American army received word at 1:00 in the afternoon from scouting parties that a large force was advancing from the north. Washington's army was caught in the middle. The battle began at 4:30 pm. After some resistance, the whole American army retreated toward the city of Chester arriving there by different roads and at different times in the night.

The next day, the American Army reorganized and marched toward Philadelphia where it was probably joined by straggling soldiers who had not reached Chester the preceding night.

On the 15th of September, Washington left Philadelphia refreshed and supplied with ammunition and marched up the Lancaster Road with the intention of meeting the enemy and again giving battle. The British commander received intelligence that Washington was advancing up on the Lancaster Road and resolved to attack him.

George Washington and troops.[33]

On the same day, the two armies met on the high ground of the Great Valley, the present site of Immaculata College. This engagement was interrupted by heavy rain which damaged the ammunition so the soldiers were unable to fire their guns. This battle was called "The Battle of the Clouds."

The American army left the Great Valley about four o'clock in the afternoon and headed northward to the Yellow Springs, about five miles distance. There, they camped for the night.

General Anthony Wayne who was ordered to harass and annoy the enemy had camped for the night in Paoli. Wayne's army was attacked with swords and bayonets while sleeping. Fifty soldiers were massacred by the British army. This incident is known as the "Paoli Massacre."

While at Yellow Springs, Washington called in a local captain, John Ralston, to guide his exhausted men to the relative safety of the south branch of French Creek. This was in the heart of his munitions makers: the Redding and the Warwick Furnaces.

It was a cold stormy day without rain when the army left Yellow Springs on the 17th of September marching through Kimberton toward Phoenixville. The army turned left on Nutt Road (Route 23) marching halfway to the furnaces by dark. They rested part of the night on Ridge Road in Vincent Township near the East Vincent United Church of Christ. Having started again at four in the morning, the long files of foot soldiers, wagons, guns and caissons began to fill the narrow valley of the south branch of the French Creek.

Washington was prepared to defend these furnaces had the British dared to penetrate the forest so deeply.

It was quite clear that Washington was figuring on all the reinforcements he could muster from Maryland, Delaware and New Jersey. He was intent on blocking Howe from reaching Philadelphia.

A storm had chilled the air to the point of light frost on the morning of September 19, 1777. The troops were still without much of their baggage due to the short supply of teamsters. The army moved eastward on Nutt Road turning left toward the Schuylkill River.

At Parker's Tavern was one of the more shallow fords, yet the water was high and full of debris from the storm.

Schuylkill River near Parker's Tavern.

The crossing would be breast high and tricky over the shoals. The army stripped to cross, holding their weapons and powder wrapped in their clothes above their heads and struggled through the strong current to the east side of the Schuylkill River.[34]

After crossing the river, Washington stopped at the house of Mordecai Evans.

Mordecai Evans house where George Washington stopped after crossing the Schuylkill River to dry off. Original house is to far right with door. [35]

The General came inside and dried his breeches before one of the two fireplaces and wrote a letter to the President of Congress describing the situation and his plans:

"I am now re-passing the Schuylkill at Parker's Ford with the main body of the Army, which will be over in an hour or two. The water is deep and rapid. General Wayne with his Division under his command is in the rear of the Army which will join us tomorrow or next day. Then I expect General Smallwood and Col. Gist with their corps. As soon as all the troops have crossed the river, I shall march them as expeditiously as possible towards Fatland, Swedes and other fords, where it is most probable the enemy will attempt to pass."

Your most obedient servant,
G. Washington

The letter was dictated by Washington and hand written by Robert Hanson Harrison. It was sent by barge to Philadelphia.

Of notable interest, before the Revolutionary War, no cannons were manufactured in the Colonies. All gunpowder was imported. Iron-masters were staunchly sympathetic to the rebellion against King George. In 1775, a Committee of Safety was formed in Philadelphia for protection. Benjamin Franklin was elected Chairman. A contract with the Warwick Furnace was made in 1775 by the Committee of Safety to cast the first cannon.

The Continental Powder Mill located on the French Creek at Rapps Dam Road, East Pikeland, was constructed to begin to make gunpowder. A smaller mill was built on the Birch Run near the village of Birchrunville.

While at the Redding Furnace, those who died either from exposure, wounds or exhaustion were buried on the hilltop. Their graves are unmarked and the site bears no commemoration. Yet, the location has been hallowed and respected for two hundred years.

A note: Years later, ashes of the campfires from colonial times were found in the area of Parker's Tavern. Also, the first men who crossed the Schuylkill River fanned out as not to be ambushed by the British troops, if any were in the area.

Parker's Tavern. Date stone on this side is 1776.

Schuylkill River Canal

In 1824 the Schuylkill River Canal made Parker Ford village part of a regional system of waterways that supplied Philadelphia with coal from the northern counties.

This scene of the canal was taken in Parkerford Pa.   (There is nothing to indicate that in the photo.)

Canal Scene Parker Ford [36]

The canal insured the vitality of the village for over fifty years. Also, a blacksmith shop in the village was contracted by the Schuylkill Navigation Company to repair its flatboats. Throughout most of the nineteenth century, the village complex remained an active center of transportation.

Bank of Schuylkill River Canal today.

Demise

Unfortunately, the source of Parker Ford's prominence being transportation, was also the source of its demise. In the late 19th and early 20th centuries the village was bypassed by the Pennsylvania Railroad. As the railroad flourished and canal trade slackened, the Parker's Ford complex was doomed to disuse and decay. Fortunately, the village refused to die. Though forgotten for decades, it continues to offer a rare glimpse at an essential ingredient, the tavern complex, in the development of transportation systems in Pennsylvania.[37]

Parker Ford Overlook on the Schuylkill River in 1900

In 1900, looking across the Schuylkill River from Parker Ford, one would see the Parker Ford Covered Bridge and the Angelo Myers Distillery.

Schulykill Bridge at Parker Ford [38]

Angelo Myers Distillery (1874 to 1918) with covered bridge on far right.

Places of Interest in Olde Parkerford Village

This is the guide of the walking tour of Olde Parkerford (Parker Ford) with historical places of interest, prepared by the East Vincent Historical Commission.

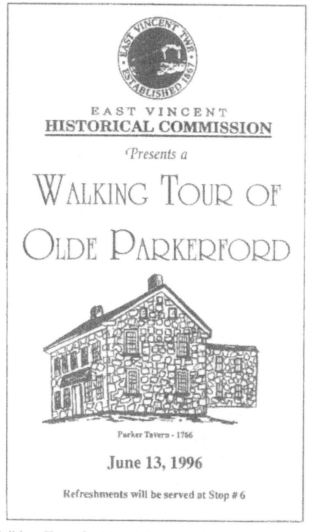

Walking Tour Guide of Olde Parkerford conducted by the East Vincent Historical Commission. [39]

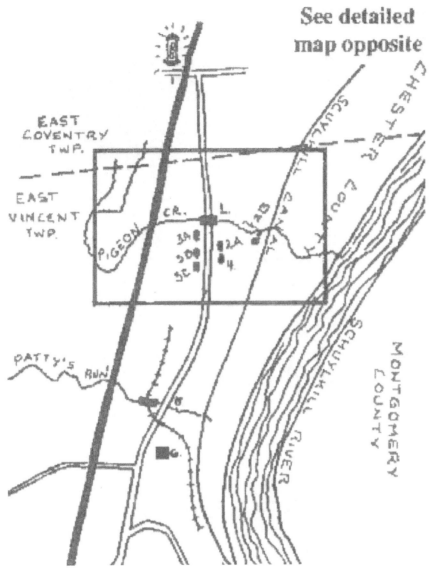

General map of the Parker Ford area.

Stop#1: Stone Bridge & Pigeon Creek Aqueduct

This aqueduct was constructed to carry the new canal over Pigeon Creek. It was constructed of heavy timbers, like a half barrel, and was held in place with stone support walls which still stand. There was a gate in the middle of Pigeon Creek and a walkway for man and donkey over the top.

Pigeon Creek Aqueduct, Parker Ford PA

Vintage Photo: Stone Bridge at Pigeon Creek Parker Ford PA

Historic Pigeon Creek Bridge (2019)

Pigeon Creek Bridge sign detail. Oldest bridge in Chester County 1804.

Pigeon Creek Aqueduct today.

Stop #2A. The Favinger House.
This two story stucco over stone colonial was once part of the early industrial complex built by Nicholas Kaiser in 1737. The house was nicely victorianized in the late 1800s, probably by Joseph T. Favinger.

Stop #2B. The Nicholas Kaiser Grist Mill Complex.
The original grist mill and saw mill were built in 1720 and rebuilt around 1800. The cider mill and blacksmith shop were built between 1847 and 1850. The foundations of these two structures are by the mill race which runs close to the north side of the Favinger house. Later, Isaac Kolb, operated a boat yard at this place. All these buildings have long since vanished from the landscape but they have left a heritage of industrial prosperity as testimony to those early German and English settlers who lived here.

Stop #2C. The Tavern Stables.

The large two story, stucco over stone colonial, built for use as a barn and stable, was able to accommodate 30 horses according to newspaper clippings dating to 1850. It now serves as a two family home.

Horse stables on left, next to Parker's Tavern on Old Schuylkill Road.

Stables arch detail.

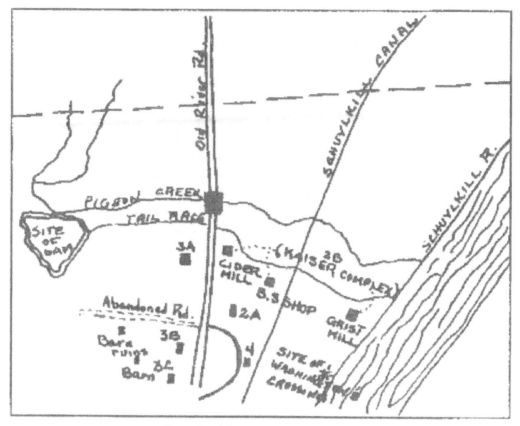

Detail of Parker Ford village.

Stop #3A. The Mackey House

This two and a half story stone dwelling was originally built as a duplex by early German settlers. M. Mackey is recognized as owner of this property in 1873 and 1883. In 1984, the main core of the house was extensively damaged by a fire and explosion. It was carefully rehabilitated, increased in size, and given a 'new lease on life'.

Stop #3B. Parker's Tavern (1766)

After the 'Battle of the Clouds' General George Washington retreated to this area, crossing the Schuylkill at Parker Ford. On his return, while waiting for the river to recede, Washington used the tavern as a temporary headquarters.

late Stone on this side 1766

Vintage Parker's Tavern

This two story cut stone colonial style tavern has a flowing spring in the cellar for cold storage. There are four rooms on each of the upper floors. The partitions on the upper floor are movable to allow for one large room. There is a crudely constructed kitchen wing with beehive bake oven in the rear of the house. Traffic from the busy canal lock, added to the everyday travel on old Schuylkill Road, creating a thriving tavern business first owned by the Edward Parker family. Parker's Tavern operated from 1766 until it was purchased by Job Fudge in 1825. Mr. Fudge changed the name of the tavern to the 'Sign of the General Pike."

"There is nothing which has yet been contrived by man by which so much happiness is produced as by a good tavern or inn."
- Samuel Johnson (1709-1784)

Parker's Tavern front view.

Stop #4: The Henry Parker House

Built in 1801, this two story stone colonial was the home of Henry and Susanna Parker, son of Edward Parker, the tavern keeper. This house, originally facing east toward the canal, was a stone's throw from the canal bed. A rehab of the house in 1932 included making the back of the house into the front. The floor plan of the house included two rooms on each floor with a fireplace on each gable end. One fireplace was used for cooking and the other for heating purposes. The 1801 stone 'lean-to' addition on the north side of the building, served as a kitchen. George Washington and his troops crossed the Schuylkill River at this point on their way back to Philadelphia in hopes to secure the fords from General Howe.

The Henry Parker House front view. The canal would have been in the
backyard. (Ann Tudors House) Not inhabited.
Built 1807. English Colonial style.

Section of Schuylkill River behind Parkers House.
Potential for a riverside trail/park.

Stop #5: Pennsylvania Railroad Aqueduct at Patty's Run

In 1870 the stockholders of the Schuylkill Navigation Company, sold their shares to the Philadelphia and Reading Railroad Company. The canal system gave way to the railroad. The rail beds were often laid on the old sites of the canal, and the prospering small canal town began to boom in the age of the railroad.

Patty Run Aqueduct, Parker Ford, Pennsylvania

The Pennsylvania Railroad was completed from Reading to Philadelphia in 1884. This line was in competition with the Reading Line (Philadelphia and Reading) to acquire a commercial stronghold in both Chester and Montgomery Counties. This aqueduct spans the narrow waterway called Patty's Run near its confluence with the Schuylkill River.

Rounding Crab Hill Cut, Parker Ford, Pa.

Canal and Railroad

Stop #6: The Webster K. Setzler Farmstead

This property is a good representation of an early farm complex, with outbuildings: the barn, barnyard with stone wall, com crib, smokehouse, stable, various sheds and the remains of a springhouse, still standing. The well kept two story brown-stone colonial farmhouse, situated near the early canal bed, is in excellent condition.

Stop #7: Canal Lock #57

Lock #57, owned by the Schuylkill Navigation Company, was engineered and constructed by Andrew Lawrence, circa 1824-1825, and for a generation thereafter the village of Parker Ford was known as Lawrenceville, in honor of the lock builder. Lock #57, the outlet lock of the Girard Canal, had a lift of 12.06 feet The level between Lock #57 and the next lock above it, Lock #56, was .85 mile, one of the shortest levels on the canal. Isaac Kolb had a store by this lock in the mid- l850s.

Lock 57 Parker Ford Pa circa 1980s

Lock 56 P. and R. Canal, Parker Ford, Pa.

Vintage photo Lock 56 at Parker Ford[40]

Indian head behind Parker's Tavern. Believed to be from Philadelphia.

Canal Lock Operation

Canal locks are a series of gates designed to allow a boat to pass from one level of water to another. After a boat has entered the lock and all gates are secured, the downstream sluices open and water flows through them.

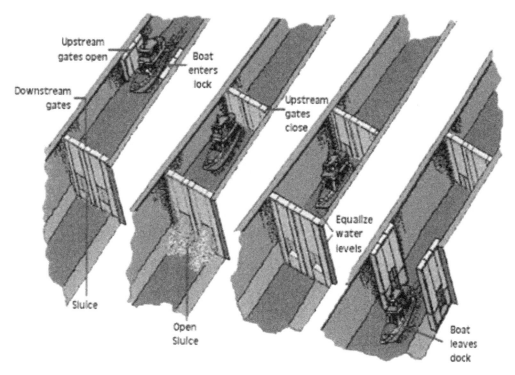

Canal lock operation.

When the water level is equal on either side of the downstream gate, water stops flowing through the sluices; the downstream gate opens, and the boat continues on at the new water level.[41]

Yankee Dam and Schuylkill Canal Scene in Parker Ford.

P. R. R. Depot, Parker Ford, Pa.

Old Pennsylvania Rail Road Depot at Parker Ford.

Chapter 4. Living With Sowbelly

For much of my adult life I have lived and worked on the family farm in view of the Sowbelly Railroad. I can see the remains of the forgotten railroad from the front windows of my home. Years ago the railroad traversed the county via the French Creek Valley. I have often walked with my children, grandchildren, relatives, and friends on the railroad embankments cut through the terrain. Several culverts, under which water once passed, and the ruins of an old stone house which stood by the tracks still remain.

Just a stone's throw downstream was the old Kennedy Swinging Bridge, supported by cables and stretched across French Creek. I can still remember how it would sway under our footsteps. Horses and wagons had to actually ford the creek, as the bridge was unable to support their weight. Further downstream embankments border the Kimberton Waldorf School. Large granite boulders on the west bank of French Creek are the only evidence of the railroad bridge that crossed the creek here.

Subsequently Howard and Vernon Rapp, who lived on their farm on Hare's Hill Road, helped their father remove the stone and ballast from the railroad line to level the land and prepare it for planting.

An abandoned railway.[42]

J.L.Beaver (1885-1973), who formerly lived on Seven Stars Road, remembered the red engine with yellow wheels. He was approximately eight years old at the time of its prominence. With the windows open during the summer, I can almost hear the old train whistle echo faintly as it takes its daily run through the French Creek Valley, reminiscent of days gone by.

Sowbelly Railroad Overview

"The Delaware River and Lancaster Railroad (DR&L) was chartered in 1868 to build a railway line between the Delaware River in New Jersey and Lancaster, PA. Construction on the line started at Phoenixville, PA at

French Creek Junction and a connection to The Pickering Valley Railroad, near Kimberton, PA. The line headed west for about 12 miles along French Creek to Saint Peters, PA. There, the DR&L connected to the end of The Warwick Branch via a switchback. Also known as the "Sowbelly Railroad", the DR&L ultimately lost money during its operation and was eventually abandoned in 1893, just 5 years after being built; the tracks themselves were pulled up a year later." [43]

French Creek Falls Station painting by Linda R. Killingsworth [44]

Beginnings [45]

The Delaware River & Lancaster Railroad which traverses the French Creek Valley crosses a section of Pennsylvania noted for its picturesque scenic beauty and for the exceptional resources of its soil.

The falls of French Creek are prominent in this respect. Also located here among the towering hills and boulders is the famed French Creek Hotel, a favorite resort for the lovers of nature's rugged beauty for more than fifty years.

The French Creek Hotel in 1910.

The operation of the Delaware River & Lancaster Railroad has now made it accessible to the general public.

Another newly accessible point made reachable by the new railroad line is Cook's Glen at Boraef Station. It is questionable whether in all of Pennsylvania there can be found any grander natural beauty.

A 1937 aerial view of the Delaware River & Lancaster Railroad Right of Way (ROW) from Cooks Glen Road crossing (left), under Sheeder Mill Farm, over Plainbrooke Farm to Wilson's Corner (right). [46]

In 1868 a legislative act authorized the Delaware River & Lancaster Railroad Company to construct a railroad from near Point Pleasant on the Delaware River to Lancaster. Its route took the railroad through southern Bucks County by way of Harleysville, through Montgomery County, into Phoenixville, Chester County and up the French Creek Valley into Lancaster in the county of the same name.

The company's board of directors met in Reading and elected Robert Crane president of the board. Also elected as directors were: Harry Carpenter, G.S Kauffman. J.K. Lineweaver, O.B. Case, R.M. Bolemius,

Alexander Seller. Samuel TasseL F.D. White, Isaac W. Guilder, Thomas Baumgardner, and Henry Smith.

The new railroad, with a total length of 47 miles, had difficulty getting started. Finally the opening date of the line arrived on November 10, 1890, nearly 21 years after the company was organized. Reports of an earlier meeting of interested parties held at Phoenixville's Temperance Hall were included in both the West Chester Daily Local and The Phoenixville Independent.

President Crane gave explanations regarding the railroad's proposed route and the prospects of becoming successful. He became actively involved in canvassing the town the following day for subscriptions to the railroad's stock. In order to begin the project immediately, $100,000 was required to be raised from Phoenixville to meet the projected expense of $8,000 per mile construction cost.

Phoenix Iron Company and Clark Reeves and Company subscribed to half of the total, or 1,000 shares, totaling $50,000. The borough was divided into four divisions and committees were appointed for each portion.

By August 5, 1873 it had become evident that the people of Phoenixville, regardless of the enthusiastic solicitation, were not buying enough shares of stock. It became necessary to hold yet another meeting to promote the railroad.

Scheduled for August 13, the next meeting appeared a bit more promising. Subscribers purchased another 350 shares, amounting to $16,650. A subsequent meeting, held in early September, took place in the Masonic Hall. That meeting provided an opportunity for Mr. Crane and other railroad officials to display a map of the proposed route.

Officials explained that large amounts of iron ore were being mined in Morgantown, Berks County. They suggested the strategic importance of the railroad, which could ship 30,000 tons of iron ore each year. Some 8,000 tons awaited shipment already.

Having purchased $50,000 worth of stock, the Phoenix Iron Company had a particular interest in the success of the rail line. Company officials also anticipated the end of the slow and cumbersome mule wagon trains which hauled the ore to the furnaces at Phoenixville.

Phoenix Iron Company Foundry Building in 1890, built in 1882.

Earlier in that year Samuel J. Reeves, president of Phoenix Iron Co., arranged to have the members of the railroad's board of directors ride over the entire route in carriages. All were in agreement that the scenery was magnificent and that it would be a terrible mistake to let the railroad slip through their fingers. However, $30,000 still remained to be raised through stock issue before the railroad construction could begin.

Construction finally began on February 1, 1883. Although it took fifteen years from the time of the initial charter, enough shares were finally issued so that surveyors were sent to stake out the roadbed. New plans had to be made for the entire line. It was decided to discard the Bucks County plans and build the railroad from Phoenixville to St. Peters, a distance of fourteen miles. Davis Knauer, owner of the iron mines at St. Peters, pushed for completion of the line so that he could ship his ore to the Phoenix Iron Co.

People of both Bucks and Montgomery Counties were disappointed in the change in plans for the railroad, as it eliminated the prospects for prosperity they had hoped it would bring to their communities.

At first plans were made to lay new tracks beside the existing Pickering Valley Railroad tracks. However, in an attempt to economize, plans again were changed and officials decided to use the existing Pickering Valley tracks from Phoenixville to Kimberton. A junction was planned for Kimberton. The name for the new branch of the Delaware River & Lancaster Railroad became the French Creek Branch.

Train at Phoenix Iron Company 1894

Junction Pickering Valley Railroad and Sowbelly Railroad at
Seven Stars Road, Kimberton PA.[47]

As the future of the railroad became brighter, surveyors were dispatched
to the western end of the line in Kimberton to stake out the roadbed.
Uncooperative landowners and threats of lawsuits slowed progress
somewhat. Right-of-way claims forced the surveyors to change the route
of the line in the area.

Other changes occurred and were recorded in a newspaper account of
1883. It was stated that the railroad may cross the state road 50 yards
south of Green's Store at the Buck, the present intersection of Route 100
and Route 23.

Heading west from Coventry the railroad was proposed to run on the high
ground above the village north of the present Methodist church and

through the old camp meeting grounds. Churches reportedly had occasional religious services outdoors in the summer months, usually under a tent.

West of Harmonyville the railroad was planned to run through a tunnel to reach an area of richer ore supply. Due to the costs involved in digging the tunnel and the influence of Davis Knauer, who had just built the Falls of French Creek Hotel, the railroad line took a more southerly route, running to the village of St. Peters.

After the delay had stretched on to twenty-one years, the Old Pottstown Ledger reported on April 12, 1889:

"...the surveying party which started on April 2 from French Creek Falls, have kept inching along until it is now as far as Kimberton."

ROW of railroad at Seven Stars Road, Kimberton PA.

The Phoenixville Independent noted on June 18, 1889 that C.A. Rice, a contractor from Saratoga, New York, was in charge of construction between the Falls of French Creek and Wilson's Corner. Alexander Palladine, a New York contractor, handled the construction between Wilson's Corner and Kimberton.

The initial groundbreaking ceremony was scheduled for Tuesday, June 18, 1889, the same day work operations began. The ceremony was held at Tyson's (Camp Sankanac) one mile east of Pughtown. There were 100 laborers, divided into two groups of fifty. One group used shovels, the other group, axes.

Contractor Rice leased four houses for his laborers, including one at St. Peters, one at Coventryville, one in Pughtown and the fourth at Tyson's Mill. Overflow workers were housed in tents.

Several years prior, in 1884, J.K. Essick, a Knauertown carpenter, erected a board shanty on the farm of Levi Bingaman at Coventryville, planning to rent it to the railroad. It is unknown whether the building was eventually used.

After seeing the benefits afforded by the railroad, landowners became more reasonable in granting the right-of-way through their properties. Several even offered free land and bought shares of stock in the company. It was certain that a station would be located and built at the mouth of the Birch Run Creek at Hall's Covered Bridge near the intersection of Sheeder and Pughtown Roads in West Vincent Township.

Sowbelly Railroad bed at Sheeder-Hall Bridge
(red covered bridge on right) on French Creek Road.

Addison Miller, owner of the Red Hill Creamery located at that
intersection, had been acquiring land and began construction on a large
stone dwelling for himself and his brother, Clinton. The brothers opened a
general store at the crossroads.

At the time land was selling for as high as $200 per acre. The Millers felt
certain that within a few years a thriving village would spring up around
them. The village never materialized.

Sowbelly Railroad in the News

The following items appeared in local newspapers:

Coatesville Affair, March 3, 1890

Josiah Keim, subcontractor, starts the erection of the trestle bridge on the
French Creek Railroad at the Falls of French Creek near Knauertown.

The bridge in front of Col. M.M. Missimer's Hotel, spanning a rocky ravine, will be about 125 feet in length.

Saint Peters trestle looking east on May 7, 2014

Another bridge over the Pottstown Road leading to Knauertown will also be 125 feet long, while the one on Samuel Kline's property and another on Mr. Murphy's property will be about 80 feet in length. When this work is done the track laying will soon begin.

West Chester Daily Local. May 13, 1890
Thus far the iron rails have been laid about a quarter of a mile from the terminus of the French Creek Railroad where it connects with the Wilmington and Northern Railroad at French Creek Falls. That part of the road is to be double tracked. Workmen are now completing the high trestle work in front of the French Creek Hotel. When this is done, the track will be laid as far as Pughtown. The wooden ties will be delivered

this week. The rails, frogs and switches for that portion of the line are at the Falls. having been brought here by the Wilmington and Northern Railroad cars.

Sowbelly Railroad bed at Pughtown.

West Chester Daily News, May 22. 1890

The only piece of grading on the French Creek Railroad yet unfinished is through the farm of R. Jones Patrick at Pughtown. This property now has been bonded and the missing links will be supplied without delay.

Contractor Davis who is bossing the track laying job, says the F.C.R.R. will be completed and ready for running by the 1st of July. There are people however who have known about the delays in building this line and will believe it when they see it so far as this of July matter is concerned.

West Chester Daily Local, June 24, 1890

Twenty-eight cars of track iron, switches and frogs for the French Creek Branch of the Delaware River and Lancaster Railroad are at the French Creek Falls, Chester County. The work of tracking the road will be pushed forward as fast as possible.

The Phoenixville Independent, 1890

A force of 60 Italian workers has commenced work on the Delaware River and Lancaster Railroad at Coventryville. They are grading on the old Revolutionary camp ground (not recorded) and have 30 horses and carts hauling earth.

West Chester Daily News, June 24, 1890

The track on the French Creek Railroad is laid from the falls to a point below Coventryville, a distance of three or four miles. The first locomotive for use on the road is to arrive at the falls of French Creek today, to be used in the work of completing the line.

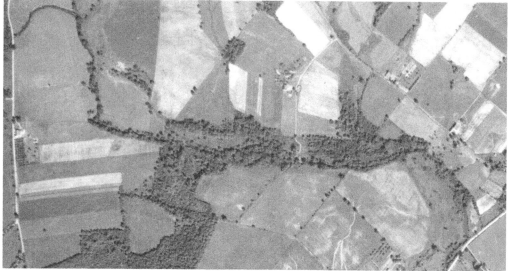

A 1937 aerial view of the Delaware River & Lancaster Railroad ROW crossing Coventryville Road (upper left corner), coming southeast across a private farmers road (center) and crossing Daisy Point Road (right) in Pughtown, Pa. [48]

West Chester Daily News, July 17, 1890
The new bridge of the Delaware River and Lancaster Railroad, 87 and one-half feet long that spans French Creek at Sheeder's Paper Mill near Pughtown, will be completed in a few days.

West Chester Daily Local, July 23, 1890
Work on the French Creek Railroad is progressing toward completion. The track is laid from the falls to Sheeder's Dam, some six or seven miles, and last grading and building on the premises of Heister and Moyer, near Kimberton was commenced today.

Coventryville Historic District[49]

West Chester Daily Local, September 17, 1890

John O. Keim who had been connected with the Philadelphia and Reading Company for nineteen years will resign his position as freight agent on Monday to accept the position of general superintendent of the Delaware River and Lancaster Railroad and will have an office at Wilson's Corner. The depot is being located at Pughtown.

Phoenixville Independent, July 15, 1890

Two parties of workers are employed in filling up and leveling the hills between Sheeder's Paper Mill and Kimberton. The number employed by contractor Rice is 75. Contractor Palladin's men number about 75. Manager Potts' men are at work at the Lockhart Farm near Wilson's Corner, and it is expected that in a short time the track will be laid. Professor George L. Maris visited the new railroad and found gangs of men at work. One gang of workers at the foot of Beaver Hill in West Vincent Township had 4 or 5 carts and 15 men.

Sowbelly Railroad bed near French Creek Road

West Chester Daily Local, September 27, 1890

Contractor of the French Creek Railroad is engaged in erection of the railroad bridge known as Millers, near Kimberton. The rails have been laid through the farm of Alexander Kennedy and the construction train runs through his property. Mr. Benton Wilson, son of James Wilson, is doing some heavy hauling with his team of horses for the contractor.

West Chester Daily Local, October I0, 1890

The French Creek Valley branch of the Delaware River and Lancaster Railroad is approaching completion and is expected to open for traffic and general business on the 18th of October. The work yet to be done is the grading of the last link, making the connection with the Pickering Valley Railroad. A bridge over French Creek below Alexander Kennedy's is still unfinished but one of the spans is built and the remainder will soon be done. This bridge has stone abutments and the balance is frame work. The freight traffic on the new line will be large because of the transportation from the extensive quarries at French Creek Falls.

Phoenixville Daily Republican, November 26, I890

The grading of the railroad is complete. Every farmer having a stick of timber that will make a railroad tie is having it made into one. By the time the railroad is completed there will not be a good stick of timber to be had in the neighborhood. The price paid by the company is 15 cents per tie.

Time	Station
-	French Creek Junction (Pickering Valley RR connection)
9:15	Heistand
9:35	Wilson's Corner
9:40	Vincent or Red Hill
9:42	Sheeder
9:45	Boreaf (Cook's Glen)
9:51	Roberts
9:55	Pughtown
10:03	Coventry
10:11	Knauertown
10:15	French Creek Falls
-	Saint Peter's (Warwick Branch connection)

Time Table for Sowbelly Railroad
French Creek Junction to St. Peter's, PA.

On December 17, 1890 the first passenger train operated between French Creek Junction at Kimberton and St. Peters. The original name of French Creek Junction was French Creek Station, located near the intersection of Township Line Road and Schuylkill Road (Route 23). There was a ceremony at the junction when the 9:15 train pulled out and residents all along the route hailed the train with flags and shouts of welcome.

A 1937 aerial view of the Delaware River & Lancaster Railroad from just below the Kimberton Waldorf School (top left edge) to where it connected with the Pickering Valley Railroad Branch at French Creek Junction north of Kimberton, Pa. [50]

The Sowbelly Railroad crossing West Seven Stars Road.

A 1937 aerial view of the DR&L Right of Way (ROW) from the quarry (upper left corner) in St. Peters Village down and across just above center, over to Coventryville (on the right). [51]

John Arnone was the line's first engineer; George Keim served as fireman; Morris Knauer became the first conductor; Sylvanus Graham was the second conductor; Clay Keim acted as baggage master, and Mr. Schaffer was brakeman.

On January 15, 1891 the train began to run on schedule. Business was beginning to boom on the railroad. Travel during the summer of 1891 was flourishing and the hotel at the falls appeared to be doing a thriving business. Davis Knauer advised the public that he was shipping paving blocks, also known as Belgian blocks, stone, and various types of granite curbing.

J.C. Roberts, a dealer in coal, feed, and lumber operated at Roberts' Station in Pughtown. Henry Mowery, manufacturer of binder boards, operated at Vincent Station. At Birchrunville, William H. Bishop dealt in groceries, general merchandise, drugs, boots, and shoes. James Murray made a living in fine furniture.

When the "Sowbelly" began running trains the cows and pigs were none too happy. The scene changed from a peaceful picture to one of noise twice daily, Monday through Saturday with trains traveling in both directions. The minute the train approached, the frightened livestock would race to the other side of the field.

Andrew Moyer, whose field the train operated, became angry and attempted to sue the railroad. He contended that the noise of the steam engine frightened his cows to the point that it actually decreased their milk production. A Chester County jury dismissed the case, saying that the suit was ridiculous.

A Sowbelly railroad car.

Delaware River & Lancaster Railroad Combine Number 1. The rail line was along the French Creek between Kimberton and St. Peters Village in Chester County, Pa. The line was operated from 1890-1894 by the Wilmington & Northern Railroad, using a leased Reading engine.

The French Creek branch of the Delaware River and Lancaster Railroad was in a flourishing condition and doing a good business. The West Chester Daily Local News of December 12, 1890 reported "The railroad from Phoenixville to Lancaster is progressing."

The Phoenixville Daily Republican account published on July 9, 1894 announced that the Delaware River railroad was to be sold. When no one bought the line, the tracks were taken up in the early 1900s.

All that remains of the railroad today are memories, cuts in the hillsides, and remains of embankments. It is rumored that the depot at Pughtown behind the Agway store was torn down and the material was used to build a barn next door, currently the Danner house. The station at Hall's bridge was moved to Birchrunville and made into a house. Most remaining stations were only platforms.[52]

Danner House and barn site of Sowbelly Railroad Station, Pughtown.

How did the Delaware River & Lancaster Railroad get it's nickname, "The Sowbelly?" No one knows for sure. Rumors suggest that because of its undulations the road bed was very uneven, with a likeness to a sow's belly. The reason for its name was suggested by my father, Walter Scheib.

My grandmother, Mrs. David Scheib, lived with her two sons, John and Charles, in Birchrunville only two miles from the railroad. Her sons frequently rode the train to the Falls of French Creek. She suggested that the name originated with the many railroad workers who came from Italy. Farmers in the area found that the workers enjoyed bacon. They quickly realized a profit when they killed their pigs and made the meat into bacon, selling it to the Italians. The German name for bacon is sowbelly. Thus, perhaps the nickname for the railroad possibly had its origin there.

Surveying and locating the western extension is rapidly done. The engineers are as far west as Churchtown in the Conestoga Valley, and a force of workers will follow to construct the roadbed. "The road will be built without a doubt."

And what was the outcome? There was never a report of any progress. The engineers and workers simply stopped work and never returned.

According to a newspaper report of the day, the railroad was a successful and profitable venture. However, it turned out to be untrue. On May 1, 1893 Chester County Sheriff J.C. Parker went to the falls of French Creek where he took control of the Delaware River and Lancaster Railroad. To recover costs, he repossessed all the track, rails and land, some of which the company actually owned. Suits against the railroad for land damage totaled some $15,000.

On July 19, 1893 the West Chester Daily Local reported that the railroad had not been paid wages for nearly three months and the laborers threatened to strike. The next four months the railroad was operated by the Wilmington and Northern Railroad. On December 2, 1893 the Wilmington and Northern withdrew its rolling stock from the Delaware River and Lancaster Railroad.

One effort was made to get the Delaware River and Lancaster Railroad line operating again. On October 10, 1894 the French Creek Railroad again began to operate and businesses along the route were delighted. Finally on November 30, 1894 traffic ceased. The railroad had been the victim of unpaid debts, law suits, sheriff levies, and a flood washout. The Delaware River and Lancaster Railroad was bankrupt and insolvent.

A 1937 aerial view of the Delaware River & Lancaster Railroad ROW from Wilsons Corner (far left) across French Creek (center) to just below the Kimberton Waldorf School (far right).[53]

French Creek Mine Number 2; Keim Mine at Saint Peters 1881[54]

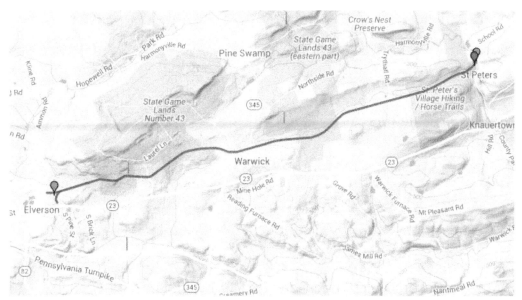

Warwick Branch - Elverson PA to Saint Peters PA map

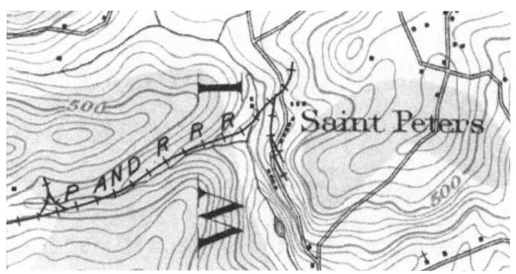

P and R Railroad at St. Peters Village 1904

ROW came closer to Old Ridge Road (Route 23) and passed through Coventryville, Pa. along Chrisman's Gristmill (1937 photo) where sidings went to graphite mines. The gristmill was later torn down for the re-alignment of Route 23. [55]

Right Of Way (ROW) of the Delaware River & Lancaster Railroad (Sowbelly) crossing Coventryville Road, looking east. (2014)

ROW of the Delaware River & Lancaster Railroad crossing Coventryville
Road, looking west. (2014)

ROW of the Delaware River & Lancaster Railroad, looking northwest,
crossing Ridge Road (Route 23). (2014)

Pickering Valley Railroad

Kimberton Railroad 1908 from Post Card

French Creek Mine 1881

Saint Peters Passenger Train Station [56]

Warwick Branch Trestle into Saint Peters on May 7, 2014

French Creek Mine Number 2 (Keim Mine) circa 1887. [57]

Chapter 5. My One Room Schoolhouse

I attended a one room schoolhouse called The Hickory Grove School in East Vincent Township from 1931 to 1939. This is an oral history with Patty Moore about my childhood school memories. [58]

Personal background, family members, family occupation

I was born way back in the year of 1925. Our family moved to a town in the adjoining township, we moved to East Vincent Township in 1926, my father, mother and my sister. And of all these years, I lived in three houses within sight of each other. My grandfather was a German immigrant. I understand he could never read nor write and they spoke German in their home. My father had a grade school education (eighth grade), but my mother had two years of high school. I went to Spring City High School and of course I completed 12 years of education. I am proud to say my four children all have their college degrees. Which I think is a great accomplishment.

Spring City High School

Spring City High School opened in 1929

My parents names were Walter and Gladys Scheib, and I was the third generation dairy farmer. My mother was a housewife. Women did not work and usually were homemakers and took care of the children. My sister Virginia sort of blazed a trail going to school. It was much easier to have an older sibling go before you because to go first you have to blaze a trail. Since I had an older sister, so she told me really what to expect.

Location and history of two Hickory Grove Schools, life during the Depression.

I attended school approximately a half a mile from my house [on Hickory Grove Road]. I started school in 1931, in first grade and I was there until eighth grade until 1939. I read in the paper about the Depression children and Depression times, I guess I was one of those children of the Depression. Most of the majority of the pupils lived on farms or small acreages. Everyone had enough to eat. The only thing we lacked was money. (We didn't know we were poor.) Money was tight. All the children had food. They were all well fed. Their clothes weren't torn or ragged; they had just common clothes, like corduroy coats. The girls all wore dresses. Slacks were unheard of. I would say that we didn't really know there was a Depression. The majority of our time was spent sledding in the winter. I don't think we had any peer pressure about buying new sleds. Usually there was a sled somewhere you could borrow or use, but occasionally a new sled would turn up.

Hickory Grove One Room Schoolhouse (1856)

The name of the school was Hickory Grove Schoolhouse. It was built in the year 1875. There was another school near this present structure. It was built in 1856. Now that may have been a private school. It was common in those times by having German background, the people could not read and write so the best next thing was to start a school and educate the children. The records are very vague but they started school in 1856 and that school was there until 1875 where it moved up to the present location.

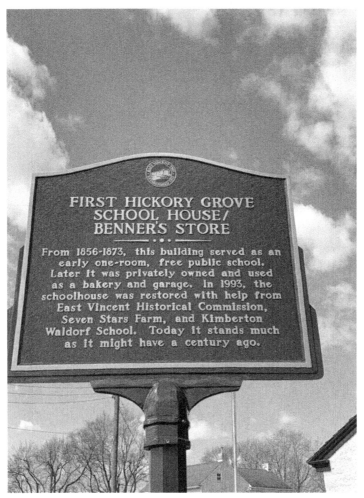

Marker Sign for Hickory Grove School House

At the time all schools conformed to the same size, before that there was a few private schools but they were all sizes and all descriptions. At that period of time, they mandated that a school be a certain size. Some had running water and some had hand pumps.

Both schools still stand today. The 1856 school, was restored by the East Vincent Historic Commission in 1992. The other school is a house.

Restoration plaque

Transportation to school, school field trips, teachers visiting the home.

I lived a mile by the road and a half a mile across the field away from home. I walked, until I was in fifth grade, and somehow I got a bicycle. Then I rode the bicycle to school. It was the family's responsibility to get the pupils to school. There wasn't a thing as school buses at the time. In my lifetime, in the 1930s, I did ride once on a school bus. The township took us and five other schools to the Philadelphia Waterworks, actually, the Fairmont Park Waterworks. We went down to see that and the seats were long ways not like they are now. They had long benches on both sides and one bench through the middle. And I remember we went on the school bus. It was the only time I went on a field trip on a school bus.

Now, there was legislation passed in 1834 that gave every child an education. It took a few years until that took effect. It took effect in larger cities, until it filtered out here. We had a lot of private schools and parochial schools. They found out those schools were teaching more religion then ABCs, so the Superintendent's position was established in 1859. His job was to make sure every school, every parochial pupil in Chester County was taught on an equal basis. Then they did have some school activities at West Chester, but I never made it to there. They primarily served our principal and administration staff.

As I was saying before, money was tight, and there were limited funds. Your school tax was the minimum. School teachers were paid very little. On that scale basis they were the same way, we were equal.

Pay was 28 dollars to 30 dollars for a week. My first two teachers, lived nearby. They lived down the road, or wherever they could board. Then they usually went home on a Saturday and Sunday. But they walked to school and it wasn't until the middle of the 1930s that our teacher came with a car.

Before that, automobiles were very slow and women didn't always drive. The cars at that time had progressed enough for the women to drive. She came every day with her old 1932 Model A Ford. I remember distinctly the year of that Ford.

Ms. Bernard was my first grade teacher for the first four years. She was our minister's daughter, so she had access to more education and maybe had the funds to get an education. She wanted to go and became the school teacher. The next one was a girl that had an automobile. A gal fresh out of college and I'm not sure we got an education at all. I mean it takes experience, but she was fresh out of college and her teaching skills weren't the greatest. I was on probation for going into the seventh year so then we got another teacher, an older more experienced teacher and she knew how to monitor and get the standards and procedures for a quality education. And she did quite well. The second teacher was Miriam Fox and the third teacher was Iva Supplee.

The teachers lived nearby. Automobiles were primitive and in cold weather you couldn't get them started so the best thing was to live nearby and a neighbor would be glad to have you as a boarder. That allowed the family another ten bucks at the end of the month, so that was great. I'm not sure I would like to live in a house and have a school teacher there all the time. Occasionally, the school teacher was invited to the pupil's homes. I recall when she was invited to my home. I had to behave myself when the teacher was there. That was something, but you survived.

School year, typical day at school, arrangement of the schoolhouse, how the teacher taught all grades in the school room, school subjects.

The school year started normally, as now, the first Monday after Labor Day. And, it usually went to the first week in May, or it depends. When I first started it was the 10th then the 11th of the month, then progressed longer then when I graduated from high school it was the 30th of May. The school year kept getting longer all the time.

The state mandates how many days that they must teach. So by this time it apparently it had to have 150 or 160 days in the school year, something like that.

There wasn't a thing called kindergarten. You just went to school, before we get too involved in this, let's talk about the school itself. When you mention a one room school, people have the idea that a teacher spoke there and taught all eight grades at one time. She did not. We started school in the morning with a salute to the flag, then we were allowed to have ten verses of the Bible to be read, then we sang songs and there was a piano in there. If the teacher could play the piano, then we had somebody to accompany us, but if not she had a pitch pipe and we sang some typical children's songs. America the Beautiful, and I'm not sure, Santa Lucia, I think we used to sing that one, my favorite, and that's the two I remember.

Enter the one room schoolhouse.

Then we started school. Then the teacher sat up front at her desk, and right in front of her desk was a bench, with a back on it. That's when she asked the first and second graders to come up, she taught combined first and second, third and fourth, so she brought the first and second graders up on the bench. There she instructed them and started, the first thing I assume she started, was teaching them how to write, and she would show her procedure how to write, then they would go back to their seats and practice their writing. Then she we ask third and fourth to come up and they would go up then she would give them fractions and so forth like arithmetic and spelling. Then after she instructed them they would go back to their seats and the fifth and sixth graders would come up, same procedure. Then when they got done she would go back to the seventh and eighth grade. That time was lunch or sometimes the end of day, but she kept rotating all of the time and some days first graders were problems. Remember it was a small school so you got individual attention. You didn't fall through the cracks.

If you had a problem, the teacher didn't to hesitate to call your parents and say he's not doing this or not writing, so you had really individual attention and another great thing about it was, I had a sister and when she got in seventh grade she loved to play "teach school". She was at the local school, so she helped the first graders. You see in every school there was a "teacher's pet", and they would come up and they would help the first graders with their writing or whatever they needed.

Some of this individual attention I remember most of the time was spelling, she would give us a word and we go up to the front of the room. There was a large blackboard across the front of the school. We would sit up there and she would give us a word and we would write it down and then she would see how we were progressing. We also did that with arithmetic.

She would give us early, three plus twelve, but then later three times four or three times squared. As we progressed she would give us this number then we would write it and do it on the blackboard and she could see how we were progressing. Mathematics was one of my better subjects, but English wasn't my greatest one. And writing, I always had poor penmanship.

We were graded on your penmanship and neatness and I never quite achieved that very good [laughter]. But that's how the teacher taught.

They had different classes like that and I would say it was quite effective, and okay.

Classroom size, clothing of school children, heating the classroom, radio communication in the school room, school directors evaluating the teacher, radio programs, school subjects, chores.

Even though there was a whole group of students from say 16-20 with varying ages and grades, individual attention was given to each of the students.

This was a farming community and it wasn't very well populated, so sixteen or eighteen, two or three in each family. I started with I think three of us, then the girls left, so one or two of us. My whole seventh grade was two of us. As I said, it was almost like a private school, because now the classes are twenty-five which is hard, but at that time it was quite easy with a small number or group. Everyone knew everyone else. And you knew everybody's IQ. You knew about what their ability was. When I went up to the board, you knew who was the one who could multiply the fastest, I guess, so everybody, and the families knew everybody, and we were all the same at that time. There wasn't anything called peer pressures. We lived and we played as children and they had clothes, some were hand-me-down clothes, nothing special. No one came with a fur coat. They did have new shoes occasionally, and girls had little long stockings and dresses. Boys had the corduroy coats, and most of the time some of the pupils wore coats and ties, or an old jacket they wore with a tie. Sometimes a tie was half way down their ankles, most of the time, and they're a little dirty from playing, but they were properly dressed. All different sizes and a lot of time you wore a sweater and corduroy pants.

A window into a one room schoolhouse

We had a large cast iron stove in the side of the room and that was the older boy's job to get out and bring the coal up. That was great to go out and bring the coal up. We had a pump and a well right next to the school, so somedays older boys did not have to go and get water at the neighbors. A friend of ours who I was discussing this about the interview, and she said she recalled two of their boys walked half a mile down the road to get a bucket of water on a pole, and bringing the water up the road and the bucket, exposed with the dirt and so forth, came up and took it into an attic container. It's no wonder we didn't die of contamination. But we were lucky we had a pump alongside the school so we washed our hands and we had individual drinking cups. Little cups that folded together, and everybody had their own cups and if it was cold enough, we could toast our sandwiches in the fire. Sometimes a fire on a cold day did not always respond. It was the teacher's responsibility to keep the fire going and sometimes it was just impossible to get that fire going. Of course we had to huddle around the stove and normally it was pretty warm. These things were a way of life, we didn't know any better.

As I sit here and look at computers today, if they had developed this or showed this at that period time, they would be absolutely dazzled at what we're doing today, this would be impossible.

Author Clyde Scheib, 2nd from right, top row, at Hickory Grove School, East Vincent Township, Pennsylvania

Our famous cartoon was Dick Tracey. Dick Tracey had a wrist--watch radio and he could talk to other people. Now, that is common, at that time that was a thing of the future. Sometime maybe you're ignorant, but we didn't have the communication, radios were old, and I recall that we finally, eventually got a radio. The biggest, not thrill, biggest objection of the teacher-- occasionally the school directors would visit the one room schools. You'd hear a knock on the door, the teacher would go to answer the door. There would be these two school directors. They would come to review her, doing her teaching methods and I don't know, but that's when she turned green and blue and everything else. She would get two chairs and they would sit back and she would continue as well as she could with her two bosses looking down at her, but they were there, it was only a matter of time; these two old gentlemen would come in and sit in the back of the room. In four or five minutes, if it was warm, [snoring sound] they were soon sound asleep. So that's what I remember, sitting back there sound asleep. But I guess they did come and observe and the teacher survived.

Oil Lamp Light

When I first started we had four oil lamps for lighting. You very seldom used the oil lamps, as I think that electricity finally came. They finally put it down the road and we got electric in the school. We had four electric lamps then we had lights, and you could see in the school on dark days. Then the radios were developed. About that time we got a radio. We had some local news and there was a music program, Dr. Damrosch, on Friday afternoons and he had a lecture on music. I don't know what the lecture was about but we had to listen to his lectures. In the meantime, that was in 1938 and 1939, that's when Adolf Hitler was over in Europe. That was the news of the day. He gave his famous speech and the Germans all cheered. We never knew what the future held at that time.

Radio was a big technological advance. We got a radio. We come home from school and we could listen to Jack Armstrong, Orphan Annie and Tom Mix. We were living and listened to Jack Armstrong, everybody wanted to be Jack Armstrong. You bought Corn Flakes to look like Jack Armstrong [laughter]. Everybody wanted to look like Jack Armstrong and Little Orphan Annie. That was our recreation and they were usually on at four o'clock so by that time we were supposed to have our homework done.

Very seldom we took homework home. Maybe to memorize a poem, something like that but very seldom we took it home because we had to walk. Sometimes they didn't always come back, but you had to memorize. We had to memorize which was never any problem with me. My problem was writing. I never was that clear and I always had some problems writing. On top of the blackboard there was an outline of all of the numbers and capital letters, and regular letters and if you got lost you could see it. Some teachers were more strict in their penmanship. Other people were more concerned about their penmanship, and now it's all computers. Some people were very particular and I had some friends who were very good in their writing. They had great writing because they were taught early in school. So the teacher was emphasizing writing. She made sure you wrote well.

Special needs children, layout of the school room, pictures of George Washington and Abraham Lincoln, getting a driver's license.

As I recall, we only had one boy that needed special attention. He had a learning difficulty. He was instructed by the teacher. He was taught how to read and write and count, but he had this learning difficulty.

We had a sandbox. If I recall somewhere we had a piano, and the piano got old so that some one made a sandbox. So we had a sandbox and he would be instructed like the other kids, but he wound up playing in the sandbox. But he graduated from eighth grade and he went on to do other things. He might have been handicapped with his math and spelling, but he certainly achieved in other ways.

So that was the only handicapped child we had in our school. His name was Sam. His eighth grade was half over and he played in that sandbox. But he didn't disrupt any of the pupils. The teacher would give him his homework and she knew his limitations. That's how she answered that problem.

In the one room school house there was a raised platform. All schools had raised platforms, and your blackboards were along the entire front of the school, and I must say we had our two heroes up there; George Washington and Abraham Lincoln.

General George Washington at Trenton 1777[59]

They were the heroes of the people, George Washington and Abraham Lincoln.

Abraham Lincoln.[60]

The smaller kids in other grades had small desks and larger ones had bigger ones, so the left hand side of the school was the smaller desks and as you advanced each year you moved up the desk so when you graduated you had a fairly decent size desk. One time they had five in the eighth grade. That was something, five in the eighth grade. That was a lot of kids and most of those went on to high school. Somehow if you wished your children to advance, you found a way to get your child to high school.

Usually it was a neighbor or someone went into town, or you just took them in yourself. Of course later on, I drove the car to school. I was sixteen and could go to the Justice of the Peace and get a license and go to Pottstown [PA] and along the street and the State Police would get in and you drove up the street and stop and turn around and come back and you'd get your license. You could drive the car. As soon as you got the permit (for two dollars), you get it taken and you'd have your driver's license that night. And there wasn't anything about insurance. Now they want minimum insurance. Well, the cars were old. Usually, the ones who came in had an old junker of a car (Model T Fords and old Chevy's) that's what the kids drove, an old beat up car. But they found ways to go to high school and the parents who wanted to encourage their children's further education found ways to get them there. My father and I took some kids in with us. I drove so it was a long way to go. If you wished to go, you could make it. My Mother didn't drive.

Attending a consolidated high school, opportunities to advance in school, going to high school during World War II, classmates who went to war, deferment from draft

I finished Hickory Grove School in 1939 and from there went into the local high school. There were three townships. I went to Spring City High School.

Spring City High School 1929-1960

The borough owned the school, but East Vincent and the other two townships were allowed to go in, and the greatest challenge was going from a one room school to the idea of transferring from one classroom to another classroom. We never were encouraged to read many books. We had an encyclopedia, but our school didn't have a library like they have now. I was never encouraged to read books. Our first English class we had to read a book in two months. That was a chore to read a book; to sit down and really concentrate on doing it. You have to get in a groove of things, that was my problem. Of course we had gym and library; just a bigger scale. The other kids from Spring City were classmates for eight years, so they were familiar with each other and so we went in, it was sort of a new ball game. But you adapted and you kind of worked through it and made it. I was in agriculture class for a couple of years and I also took industrial arts. If you wanted academic courses meant you were going to college to further your education. With secretary courses you could go to become a secretary.

After I got into high school, for the first couple of year we really didn't care about school because World War II came along and they were taking everybody there was. So why should we put up with all this English when we go be on the front lines, because you know where we're heading. Several of my classmates were older and taken out of high school. That's when they passed the law to take the eighteen year olds. Some of my classmates didn't pass a grade or got sick. If you were ill you didn't get drafted. So it wasn't because of your mentality, it's because maybe for health reasons. Some of our boys were older and they were taken into the Army.

My classmates did not enter the War in the early stages. Most of them were in the Battle of the Bulge.

Battle of the Bulge

That time they were older, eighteen and nineteen years old and were involved with the Battle of the Bulge. They had no idea when they got on that train what was ahead of them. My classmates had no idea when they left, they were just happy, lucky boys, and they never knew what they were going to hit when they got over there. They really learned fast and they learned how to survive, and most of them came back. There was only a few of them who didn't come back. Most came back and went on to become useful citizens.

I graduated from Spring City High School in 1943. That was the height of World War II. I was deferred from the draft because I was a farm boy. Food was that crucial, that the number of anybody with a certain amount of acreage and animals were entitled to stay home to produce food. So I wasn't called 'til 1945, then the war was over, so then we were done.

Activities at school (lunch, recess), discipline at school, use of ink well, school supplies.

For lunch at the Hickory Grove School, it was a paper bag from home, Brown bag-it, as they say. But we had lunch kettles. We had a tin lunch kettle, a box with a double handles on it. We had a sandwich, typically baloney, summer baloney, apple, cookies, and if the jar didn't leak too much, your mother put chocolate milk in the jar. There wasn't anything called a "thermos jug". Apples and pears were home grown. Cookies and cakes were home baked. At lunchtime we'd go outside and climb a tree, or sit on the wall, or hike the woods or something like that. We played ball and hiked and just buddy-buddy. The girls never played ball. They used to fight like you do today, boys would have disagreements and they would fight. I mean no blood like that, but they would punch each other and roll around in the dirt like that. That next day they would be best friends. I was thinking about knives, some of the boys carried knives. You could do things with them, but they got heavy and you usually lost it, so that was the end of your knife episode. I took a knife to school. Someone gave me an old knife and I was showing it to everybody and few days later I lost it. So that was the end of the knife [laughter].

Clothing, I say, we had corduroy pants, warm clothing. We didn't have central heating in the houses, so you were prepared for cold weather. So you had the long stockings and so forth and there wasn't boots, there were shoes and you wore goulashes or boots over top of them or sometimes hand-me-downs. I hear people talk about the Depression era and I lived through it, but I'm not sure how we lived through it.

Hickory Grove School circa 1936
Teacher: Ruth Bernard; Back row: Thelma Keeley, Frances Thomas,
Virginia Scheib Second row: Frank Lucas, Mike Cehula, Thomas Cehula
Front row: Alymer Thomas, Charles Shick, Charlotte Kersbergen,
RoseMarie Lucas, Marian Youngblood, Vernon Keeley, Clyde Scheib,
Donald Youngblood

That was the extent of a day of our school. We had 8:30 start at school,
10:30 was recess for 15 minutes. That's when you could go to the
bathroom and get a drink of water or snack, then lunch was between 12
and 1 o'clock. We had some neighbor boys. They walked home. They
were a farm family and they walked home for lunch and they never
brought their lunch. They always walked home. And, incidentally, I should
say they're the boys who, would catch and trap for muskrat or skunks,
and things like that for extra money. Apparently that morning they caught

a skunk and they came to school without changing their clothes and when they came in the door, the teacher sent them home to change their clothes cause they smelled that bad. Of course they were used to the smell, but when they came into the school, the teacher said "get out of here" and I remember when she chased them home to change their clothes from the skunk smell.

If some of the boys were misbehaving on the playground, the teacher disciplined you by slapping you. She didn't go out and get you, but usually she stayed in. As I say it was sort of a close knit community with the families. If the teacher would happen to hit me, they usually slapped your face. They got your collar and they'd slapped your face. If the teacher did that to you, you didn't go home and say "mommy, teacher hit me".

That's one of the disadvantages of having an older sister in your school. Guess what? Your sister would go home and as soon as she got into the door, "Guess what? Teacher hit Johnny!" That's when the mother and father got involved [laughter]. So you made sure that you kept in line. You were there to learn and be educated. You weren't there to cause trouble. If the teacher had struck me, I wouldn't go home and talk about it. But, sisters are one to tattle tale and go home and tell your parents.

The emphasis was on education. You were going to school to learn, not to horse around, not to play and carry-on. The idea and the emphasis was education, to better yourself. It's still the same way today. People are still scrimping and saving to send their kids to get a higher education. They think it's that important so really it hasn't changed in all these years.

As a student at school, I was disciplined one time as I recall, the teacher hit me one time. I don't know what for [laughter]. She got me going to the door, and I don't know what that was for. She slapped you. The only time I remember, she slapped the kids. She didn't beat 'em up like that or use wooden sticks like that. There was no way. She might slap their fingers, or they were doing something like that, but this old story of pigtails in the inkwell, I don't think it every existed. She didn't give you ink. You didn't have ink. That was expensive. When you got older, you were capable of using ink, then she would give you a Waterman ink bottle.

1930s Waterman ink bottle

Then you would draw with this ink. You had ink all over the place, and not like the fountain pens you have today. That ink, they would drop ink everywhere, and that would stain. It depended upon your teachers. Majority of the teachers were very confident, and if you wanted to learn, it was there. If you didn't want to observe it, that was your problem. It was there like today. The teachers are there. The system, if the kids want to learn, it's there. If they don't, then that's another story.

As far as school supplies, we were only supplied extra pencils by the school. There was a thing in those days, "school companion". A little cardboard box: it had a ruler, extra crayons and a couple of pencils. But the school provided you all the paper and pencils you needed. And a pencil sharpener, boy you could spend all day sharpening a pencil [laughter]. Teacher would say "you sharpened that enough, sit down" [laughter]. Cause some kids had a habit of always walking back to the pencil sharpener. "I broke my point", and some of the kids had the habit of breaking their point quite often. Typical, typical.

School and home chores, knowledge of growing up during the Depression, social events at the school including birthdays, Thanksgiving, Christmas and Valentine's Day, end of school party.

Of course you always had the teacher's pet that always hung around the school. The only chore was sweeping out the school, and sometimes volunteers would do that.

I know by living on a farm, we had farm chores to do. You had the wood box to fill. You had other chores to do when you got home.

You had some animals to attend to, so you did not stay at school. I know my chore was filling the woodbox up at home. When I got old enough I never was going to have a fireplace and cut any more wood, but now I've got a fire place and I'm still cutting wood. But of the chores, you didn't stay at the school. Most of the kids went home and did their farm chores and cared for animals. And that was just part of your growing up experience.

We really did not discuss world events or politics during school. Up through eighth grade and even to twelfth grade, you didn't discuss too much about it. In the Depression, people were concerned about surviving. As I say, there was just a shortage of money and you were lucky to have a house. If you had a warm house, enough to eat, and a fair amount of clothes, and you weren't concerned about it. Of course when we were young we worried about playing and skating and things like that. But we did have social events. We had birthday parties. The kids would have birthday parties. I know one boy got a Mickey Mouse watch. Boy, he was lucky. That was peer pressure. I was lucky. He got a Mickey Mouse watch. I bet it cost two dollars, for his birthday. That was living, [laughter] that was living. We would play and visit each other and play, as today, you don't need constructive toys. You made your own toys and games. You played and ran and made houses and built houses and all kind of neat things. When you are living in this, you don't realize what you're living through. And as I say, the only thing I remember is Adolf Hitler talking on the radio, other than that, maybe some of the men had talked about it. I think the most important part, we were coming out of the Depression when World War II started and people went to work. Everybody had jobs, and before that young men couldn't get jobs, but then they started to go to work that's when newer automobiles turned up, and people could buy radios. That was the extent of it as I recall.

Holidays like Thanksgiving was just an event at school. You made pilgrims and so forth, and you had your Thursday and Friday off, and a Saturday and Sunday. Christmas was a bigger thing because we had a Christmas performance for the families. Of course that meant that we had recitations, plays, sing some songs. And a different story, my remembrance of the two girls had a play about baking a cake, and the expression was it said in the book, "separate two eggs". So, they put one egg on one side of the room and the other egg on the other side of the room, so they separated the eggs. Of course that was a funny thing.

Then we sang. All the families came and of course they all clapped and half of us couldn't carry a tune. It was kind of corny but it was one of those social things. The parents, if they were involved with the school, had a PTA meeting once or twice a month. Being this close-knit family, they got together at different events. And they used to go play cards. Somebody went and bought a gallon of oysters.

Gallon of Oysters

Of course we had the milk from the farm, so we had an oyster stew supper because we had the milk. That was when you could afford to buy a whole gallon of oysters. Somebody got a couple of dollars and they brought oysters, so all the neighbors together with us, maybe fifteen or eighteen of us got together.

So that was one of the activities at school, and of course Valentine's Day was another big day. We had a Valentine box and we made them. If you got a store bought Valentine, you were living [laughter]. Most of the time you went out and took a piece of blank paper and you would draw a thing on that or put something on it. And the girls that wrote them mushy things and the boys they just put "Valentine's Day" and put it in the box. And of course they had a big square box and they would open it up and they gave you the Valentine. Usually you got a Valentine for everybody.

Someone would receive a book, a ten cent book, cutout ones. They were living.

At the end of the year we had a picnic on the last day of school and some of the parents came in. The men would come in and eat lunch and would go home and the women would stay and talk. Then we played and then sort of that was the end of the school year.

Then we survived all summer. The hardest part was going to school in September. Now, everybody went barefooted. Boy, everybody went barefooted. Did you ever go barefoot all summer then had to put a pair of shoes on? And sit in school for a couple of hours? Oh you couldn't wait to get out of school and get your shoes off [laughter]. Isn't that right? Yeah. Everybody went bare footed like that, and put those shoes and go back to school and put those new shoes on, oh that was torture and you'd get out of school and everybody took their shoes off and walked home.

We walked by an apple tree, and we used to stop and eat the apples off that tree. Boy, were they delicious. They were the best apples in the country. Now if you could go back in time,and take an apple off that tree, you would be highly disappointed. They don't taste nearly as good as they did then. So, that was my walk home from school.

School courses, activities in the classroom, memories of helping elderly neighbors, report cards, quality of high school graduates

In addition to the core courses, such as art, music and drama, we also drew pictures. As I say, it depended upon the teacher. Sometimes she would emphasize art, and she would give you coloring pages and you had a crayon within a certain line, and so forth. Minimum, we had reading, writing, and we had geography. Geography taught you about the world. History was mostly George Washington and Abraham Lincoln, cause they were the martyrs up there. Lincoln's picture was on this side and Washington's on the other side. We didn't have the modern heroes we have now. Maybe there weren't that many of them, but that's what was involved at that time.

Of course there was the flag. I think at the end of school the teacher took the flag down. And of course we had the pledge of allegiance. Then when she realized it was time, at almost 3:30, realizing we didn't have a clock. There wasn't anything like a clock like that, you knew when the teacher started to do certain things that it was time to go. She told you "time to put away your books", so you put away your things like that, and the schools excused. You went out, you walked out. You didn't run out. You didn't run through the school. You walked in like ladies and gentlemen. You didn't run in or run out like that. If you ran, you wouldn't run the second time, after being disciplined. And of course in your lifetime you knew teachers who disciplined more then others. You know, some teachers you didn't breathe when you were there [laughter]. Other kids told you about what your teacher was like, so you knew what to do, so you didn't cause trouble. We didn't know with all these things, we never knew what we were supposed to do, until you read about them.

Another interesting thing. On the way home from school, there was an old house. A brother and sister lived in the house. My father took us to school, and of course they were older; I bet they are a lot younger then I am now; but they were older and he would stop by and they lived in the house and they didn't have any car, telephone and anything like that, just lived in the house. So the sister wasn't feeling well one night, and my father said, "if you ever need any help, put your light in the window". So, remember there wasn't any electricity. It was all dark. So, one night he went to bed about nine o'clock and he looked back and saw the light in the window.

He got dressed and went back. Apparently she had gall bladder trouble or something like that. Of course they got her in the car, I don't know where they went, but they went and knocked on the door and the doctor got up and said "What's the matter?" Apparently she had a gall bladder attack or something like that, and it wasn't fatal or anything.

But then he took her back home, and that was the way of communication at that time, it's how they looked after neighbors. People still have a tendency to look after the elderly. Well they did then too. They knew older people and they sort of stopped and asked, "What do you need?", like that and they'd get it for them, or just watched out for them. So, we watched out for that family. Of course they both passed away later on, and that was the end to it.

Progress was evaluated every year at school. You always had a report card. And you had to sign it. Every six weeks you got a report card and you would put on your grades and so forth, like that. Also, sometimes I got a "B", mostly it was "C", and sometime I got a "D". Especially penmanship [laughter].

Neatness and penmanship and that was a little curriculum on the side. Reading and writing and arithmetic. History. Geography. SocialStudies. Whatever she could sort of work in like that. I say, it all depended upon the teacher. She was taught how to do these things. If she had more intelligent kids, I'm sure she could progress faster. But she had all kinds.

She just put them all together. As I would say, we got a basic education. If I recall, the United States industry was run until about 1960 by high school graduates. All the factories after World War II were run all by high school graduates. Then of course we got more knowledge and college degrees.

Before that most of the people that ran these big factories had mere high school educations. And they did quite well, in my estimation. As I say, the older, or the more kids with a little more intelligence and needs that wanted to go, like my sister, went to business school. She was more intelligent then I was. I didn't care. Boys, they just went to school and had a good time.

Other one room schools within township, comparison of education before and after consolidation of the elementary schools, education is all about what you make of it, "we weren't poor; we just didn't have any money", thankful for good health

There were other one room schoolhouses in the area in operation at the same time as Hickory Grove Schoolhouse. There were seven in the township. You walked to your schools. There wasn't anything like public transportation. You walked to school.

Usually they were a mile apart. You had to walk within a mile. You can go either way. If you were on the border you could go to any school in the township. We were in this end of the township. Some villages were closer together but this end; we were sort of on the boundary lines. There were only five of us from this edge of the township that walked up to the school. The rest of them were from Route 23 which was more populated. There was more houses on Route 23, so there were more kids that came down. Of course there was a larger family up there. The family had seven kids so naturally there was more of these.

After World War II, the consolidation came in. Some townships were lucky to have a beneficiary to put in consolidated schools. Other townships had just taxpayer's money.

And the house we're in, the school near there, the Kimberton Waldorf School, that school was a donation by a wealthy industrialist. So he gave them money to build this expensive twenty-eight thousand dollar school. And the first time it was proposed to the tax payers, they turned it down because they couldn't afford it. But two years later he came back in with four more thousand dollars and they put the school system in.

We had school directors, but there wasn't any money to expand the education to all the schools. Like I said, they were all named and until then the jointure came in the 1950s. But before that our township had a consolidation and we put all schools together. Before the consolidation, one district bussed the kids to individual schools.

So instead of having eighth grade they only had two grades per school, so that way they got ready for the jointure. It was a process. Sometimes after these things are proposed, it took a few years until they got into affect. Surprising how well everything turned out.

We may growl about school taxes. It's amazing how this all happened to the schools. We can all know why, because some of these older people must have had an insight. But it was just a process of education.

Comparing the education I received in a one room schoolhouse to others, including my children, who all went to a consolidated school, I must say education sometimes doesn't always mean how intelligent you are.

People you think that are highly educated, sometimes I can say, and you've heard it before, they're too dumb to come in out of the rain. Other people with minimum education have exceeded quite well. They've gotten prosperous and have companies and have prospered quite well. So it's hard to say about different types, it all depends upon the individual. If you wish to excel and do all the things you can or if you didn't want to or don't care. It all depended upon the families. The families were involved with you. They made sure that you were learning. They didn't just put you on the school bus and they went to work. They were involved where you went to school.

You took your books home and they usually looked at your book or say something like, "Where are you at?" If you had any trouble, the school teacher didn't hesitate to call your parents up and tell you "Johnny's having trouble". I think he should do some homework, or you better put him to bed earlier". Just things like that which helped, which I don't think we have today.

I think that education, it's there and I think the kids have to sort on their own to absorb it or not absorb it. Children don't always have the ability to decide what's good for them.

In closing as I say, we were poor, no we weren't poor; we just didn't have any money. But we weren't poor, we had food and clothing. This is the way that period of time was. And as I say, I have no regrets, and certainly in my life I could have studied a bit more, and a better vocabulary, and maybe learned how to concentrate more.

School teaches you how to concentrate and when you don't have that background, you do other things. I could not go back to school. I couldn't concentrate. I couldn't focus on doing that. You have to sort of get early training. But I have no regrets and it was a time I lived through. I just hope, and that I'm thankful I have lived this long that I can share and give insight into what I remember and somebody else might have a different interpretation.

I am just thankful. A lot of my friends have passed away. I have a school photograph; three quarters of those have passed away. And I'm still thankful that I can do this and have my right mind. As you get older you get senile. As I say, I enjoyed going to school. A lot of memories, and I don't think I'll ever have another chance to do it [laughter]. I think one chance only. That's the way it is. [61]

Chapter 6. Underground Railroad in Kimberton

The following are stories I have heard and written about are local folk lore of the Underground Railroad in my many years living in the Kimberton, Pennsylvania area.

By the 1900s, it was common knowledge what happened in the old Kimberton Girls School (Kimber Hall).

At the general store across the road much was discussed about the School and its involvement in the trackless Underground Railroad. Stories of tunnels, secret rooms, ground cellars, a lit room in the upstairs, carriages coming in the middle of the night with overheated horses and muddy wagon wheels. Stories of quilts with a direction printed on them and hung on an outside clothesline.

Beginnings

For centuries African tribes raided neighboring villages capturing the men and women and keeping them as prisoners of war, then selling them to the Spanish ship captains and taking them to the West Indies and the United States to work on Southern Plantations. One fugitive seeking freedom, thought he had walked so far but learned later that he had walked only eight miles from the Mason-Dixon line.

Once the fugitives crossed the Mason-Dixon line, other freed African American families living in Southern Chester County gave them lodging and helped find a place of employment.

A driver taking a load of wool to the Charlestown Wool Factory on the Pickering Creek delivered two fugitives to Emmor Kimber in Kimberton.

DANIEL GIBBONS.

HANNAH W. GIBBONS.

Daniel and Hannah Gibbons, both members of Society of Friends. [62]

Daniel Gibbons (1775-1853) lived near Bird-In-Hand in Lancaster County. When the fugitives were taken from the barn in the morning to the house, each one was asked his name, the name of his master, what part of the country he came from. These questions with the answers to each were recorded in a book which gradually swelled to quite a volume. After passage of the Fugitive Slave Law, Gibbons burned it.

RESIDENCE OF DANIEL GIBBONS.

Residence of Daniel Gibbons

When a company of African American people came to the house, they were asked whether they expected their master soon. If not they would get work in the neighborhood for a while. If the master was expected in a short time, it made it necessary for them to hasten on. They would be moved on as soon as possible. If the house was to be searched with or without a warrant, fugitives were taken to the corn field to hide in a corn shock and remained until danger had past.

The enactment of the fugitive-slave law in 1850, a gang of negro informers headed by a well known character near Gap, west of Coatesville, Pa. scoured the country side ready to seize upon any African American person and put them in chains for a life long slavery for a ten dollar ($10.00) bounty. Before the Civil War, the Kennett Square

(Southern Chester County) abounded in free African Americans and Society of Friends (Quakers) with it's abolitionist population and it's location just a few miles north of the Mason-Dixon Line. Here was a hotbed of abolitionist became a magnet for fugitive slaves, a place where freedom seekers were sure to find food, clothing, refuge and encouragement. [63]

Road to Freedom

Follow the North Star to freedom according to folklorists spirited songs "Follow Drinking Gourd" or the Big Dipper encouraged them to flee to the north. For those who did achieve the dream, there were many reasons for running away. Among the most common was the death of a master and subsequently being sold, separating the families.

Most of the ones to flee were young males without families and without responsibilities. Fear of separation, families left in groups.

Fugitive slaves undercover 1850.[64]

Most runaways left in the warmer months of the year. Food could be found in small game, fruits and wild vegetables. Many who fled came from Delaware, Maryland or Virginia. There were never any records of how many they were or where they started from. Questions were never asked. At an Underground Station, in the middle of the night a group or single fugitive was ushered in the door. The women quickly prepared a meal, fed them, clothed them or gave them water to wash. Then they were taken to a secret room, or to the barn, or to an African American neighbor so not to arouse suspicion. Not much was said, just action. When it was safe, they were taken to the next station.

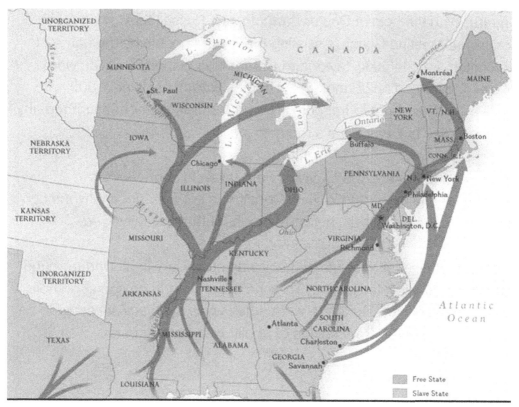

Underground Railroad network for enslaved African Americans to obtain their freedom. [65]

Wilmington, Delaware and Kennett Square

Wilmington was one of the hubs of trade, commerce and social life. Plantation and land owners from Delaware, Maryland and Virginia came to Wilmington for business, or social and the holidays. With the masters came the slaves as drivers, personal servants or helpers. Slaves were told by friends if they could find a Quaker who was wearing a broad brimmed black hat and suit, maybe they could help them flee to the north.

A Quaker by the name of Thomas Garrett could help them. On finding Garrett, he could get arrangements made to transport them to Kennett Square. With the help of Doctor Bartholomew Fussell they could reach Longwood Meeting House. Assisting them were people by the name of Darlington, Mendenhall, Taylor and Barnard; all of these families were involved. Between 1822 and 1863 Thomas Garrett assisted 2,300 fugitives on their flight to freedom. Thomas Garrett never encouraged any fugitive to flee but was always ready to assist.

From Kennett Square, the fugitives were taken to John Vickers in Lionville, and Micajah and William Speakman in West Vincent. Not much is known of the Speakman activities or where they actually lived.

Another myth is that absolute secrecy was necessary in all Underground operations. Abolitionist such as Thomas Garrett made no secret of their work aiding fugitives. But there were times when such activities had to be carried out in secret. Reputations of abolitionist were generally well known.

John Vickers

John Vickers was a Quaker when he married in 1823, purchased a farm in Lionville, and continued in the manufacture of pottery. Like other stations and abolitionist, a knock on the door in the night hours, the

186

women arose and prepared a good meal for them. Then they were scattered around various places, until they were ready to move on.

JOHN VICKERS.

John Vickers illustration. [66]

After the Fugitive Slave Law was passed in 1850, John Vickers did not keep any fugitives about his premises but always sent them to a tenant house occupied by an African American man, Josh Robinson.

Dr. J. K. Eshleman in Downingtown, PA. became involved in the Underground Railroad in 1840. Dr. Eshleman received fugitives from Chester and Lancaster counties and sent them to John Vickers. Dr. Eshleman's children saw African American people in the house frequently but they were not permitted to ask any questions or know anything about them. The Doctor spoke of his activities only to a very few friends.

John Vickers, when delivering wares in his wagon hid slaves between the boxes. When the fugitives were moved on, sometimes they were given a note for passage, with the words "thy Friend Pot". Vickers never lied when questioned about fugitives.

Residence of John Vickers [67]

Norris Maris

Norris Maris lived and worked on the Lewis Farm and assisted the fugitives. He purchased a farm in 1854 in the Kimberton area (Pughtown and Chester Springs Road). Maris was usually the driver of the carriages or wagons that transported the fugitives.

NORRIS MARIS.

Norris Maris lived on a farm near Kimberton PA. [68]

If Maris was unavailable to transport the fugitives, Vickers would give them directions. They were near the Maris home when they could smell pomace (apple skins) from across the road at Abraham Buckwater's Cider Press.

Maris son, George, a young man of ten drew a map of the road for them to reach Elizabeth Pennapacker's place.

A young man with two fugitives going down a road to work caused no concern to the neighbors.

Pikeland Meeting House

A group of eleven families partitioned the Goshen Meeting House and established a meeting house and cemetery in Kimberton area called

Pikeland in the year of 1758. As the slave issue strengthened, Pikeland became a progressive meeting house. Members started to participate in anti-slavery meetings and movements.

Disagreement between the members formed two factors. One for slavery and the other remaining uninvolved. Hicksite Quakers became involved in the movement and the Orthodox remained neutral.

The split between the Hicksite and Orthodox caused Emmor Kimber to build a new meeting house near his school on Pughtown and Cold Stream Road, later to become the Lutheran Church. Other Quaker members were Fussell, Thomas, Rogers, Star and Meredith, to name a few.

Rachel Harris

A slave girl named Rachel Harris owned by a man in Maryland, made her way to Emmor Kimber. The family being in need of a servant, employed her as a cook for a long time. She married later and moved to Minor Street in West Chester.

Rachel had a lively, clear and strong musical voice. As she sat in her doorway in the evening and sang, she was heard in all parts of town. A large reward had been offered for her return and a man in West Chester learning of this, engaged a constable and came to arrest her, and took her before the judge.

While the examination was going on in the judges office, Rachel asked permission to step out into the backyard, which was granted. Outside she scaled the seven foot fence and escaped, up the alley to Dr. Worthington's house. She asked "Please for God's sake, take me in" and immediately she was taken in and up to the garret, hiding her in a cubby hole, fastened the door and returned downstairs.

The Constable exasperated at her escape went back to his office. That evening at dinner at Dr. Worthington's house, there was no sign as to what happened or that anything unusual had occurred.

Emmor Kimber (1775-1850)

Emmor Kimber's house was a welcome refuge to all who sought his aid. Kimber, a teacher at Westown Friends School near West Chester bought the grist mill, Kimber Hall and general store sometime in 1817. Emmor Kimber established the "French Creek Boarding School for Girls". The school opened in 1818 with his daughters Abigale, Martha and Gertrude. Emmor Kimber was Superintendent.

French Creek Boarding School for Girls in Kimberton 1900-1920.

The school became known for its English, drawing, painting and French language studies. Students came far and wide, coming in carriages and stage coach. Prominent iron families included Brooke, Lykens, Rutters and Pennapacker attended. Tuition and boarding for six months was $75.00. When Kimber died the Underground activities ceased.

Kimber did not want to violate the Anti-fugitive Slave Law which made it illegal to hide other men's property.

Kimber is buried in the private burial ground in front of the main entrance of the Kimberton Lutheran Church. In 1897, the Kimber family deeded the cemetery to the church.

Did the parents of the students of Kimberton School know that Kimber was an abolitionist? Nothing was discussed about what happened in the cellar or barn on the farm. The farm today consists of the Valley Dell development and Miller's Pond.

French Creek Boarding School for Girls - 1937

The school building has enlarged with many rooms, large and small with many places to hide someone. A tunnel dug from the school would arouse suspicion. Having African American farm hands to work the fields would arouse little suspicion. Two African American men with hoes or rakes walking down the road unnoticed, but on their way to freedom.

Abigal Kimber became a teacher at her father's school at the age of fourteen. She enrolled herself in the Anti-slavery Society. She was Vice-President and Recording Secretary of the Philadelphia Female Anti-slavery Society and a delegate to the London, England world convention in 1840.

Lewis Family

John Lewis was born in West Vincent Township, Chester County in 1781. He was a member of the Pikeland Preparative, Uwchland Monthly and Caln Quaker Meeting. John Lewis married Esther Fussell and had six children, notable Graceanna Lewis. Their home was not merely a station where the fugitive could be received and fed, but it was a home where the sick and over fatigued were kept and nursed until they were able to proceed again.

On one occasion forty fugitives passed on the Road to Freedom. Some of the men were put to work on their and neighbors farms. When the sick and weary were sufficiently restored and able to leave, Norris Maris and others frequently took them to Emmor Kimber and onto E.F. Pennypacker station at Corner Stores, or on to Lewis Pearts, Audubon, Montgomery County. Some were placed on the Reading Railroad to be taken to Canada. Those had to be well dressed to give the appearance of normalcy to elude the searching eyes of the slave owners.

Large quantities of exquisitely clean and mended clothing were sent to the station. Clothing collected by friends living in Pottstown and

Lawrenceville, and others by the descendants of John Price living in Pottstown.

Graceanna Lewis

Look at Graceanna Lewis. No casual observer would have suspected her as the operator of a station of the Underground Railroad. She and her sisters, Marion and Elizabeth looked the part. Yet they operated one of the busiest stations for slaves fleeing from the south.

GRACE ANNE LEWIS.

Graceanna Lewis (1821-1912) illustration. [69]

Frequently professional slave hunters suspected the Lewis girls. Graceanna permitted them to search the house, barn and farm.

Graceanna set one restriction "no gentleman would peer into a lady's bedroom", she told searchers.

Graceanna Lewis marker in Kimberton, Pennsylvania [70]

After the ending of the Civil War, Graceanna started to paint and draw, studying at the Philadelphia Academy of Natural Science, painting flowers, plants, animals and birds. After she and her sister inherited the farm from her father, she operated and sold iron ore from the farm to the Phoenixville Iron Company (1830-1833). One thousand tons of ore was sent from the mine. Graceanna died in 1848.

Doctor Bartholomew Fussell

DR. BARTHOLOMEW FUSSELL.

Doctor Bartholomew Fussell, member of Society of Friends.[71]

Dr. Fussell was born in West Vincent Township. At the age of sixteen he moved to Maryland and decided to study medicine. He taught by day and read for his profession at night. He set up practice at Kennett Square. He attended the Anti-slavery convention in 1833 in Philadelphia.

Dr. Fussell labored with Thomas Garrett of Wilmington, Delaware in assisting 2,000 fugitives on their way to freedom. He was a member of the Longwood Progressive Meeting House. Dr. Fussell died in 1871. He and his wife are buried in the Pikeland Friends Cemetery, Kimberton, PA.

Elijah Pennypacker

Elijah Pennypacker owns and resides on part of a large farm owned by his father in Schuylkill Township, Chester County. He was a member of the State Legislature for four sessions and Secretary of the Schuylkill Canal Board. He joined the Society of Friends at Corner Stores about a year after his retirement from political life. Pennypacker was active in anti-abolition movement and assisted many on their way to freedom.

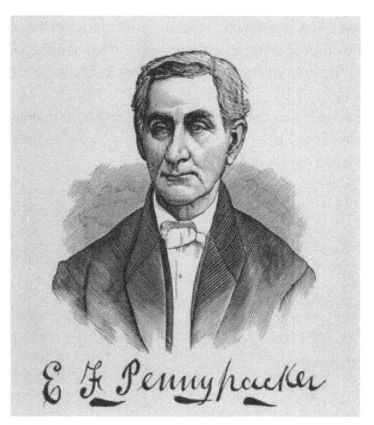

Elijah Pennypacker [72]

The residence of Elijah Pennypacker was the most eastern station in Chester County and the point where the three most important routes converged. One route having its starting points in York, Adam and other counties, passing through Lancaster, Columbia and northern Chester County. The second route passing through the middle of Chester County and the third, starting at the same points but passing through Kennett and Willistown. From Elijah Pennypacker the fugitives were sent to Norristown, Quakertown and Philadelphia. Some crossed the Schuylkill River in paddle canoes at Pauling's or Port Providence. Elijah kept a large two horse Dearborn wagon in which he took loads of fugitives by day or night. If they reached his house in the night and there was an urgency to proceed, they were taken on without delay. In case they were taken in day time, the women and children were placed in the rear end of the wagon, the children were covered up and the women disguised by wearing veils. The men walked singularly as not to excite suspicion.

Pennypacker lived to see national slavery abolished. He maintained his vigor and his testimony against liquor and beverage. At his death he is buried near the Corner Store Meeting House. [73]

Chapter 7. Bonnie Brae Park

Bonnie Brae Park, Spring City, Pennsylvania

Klan Origins

The original Ku Klux Klan (KKK) terrorized the South between 1866 and 1872. The Klan was started by an ex-Confederate, Colonel Livingston, in Mississippi who thought the law was too unjust and who took the law into their own hands. By the end of the 20th century, the Klan had almost vanished. A few Klansmen met and remained as a social club.

It was a warm, muggy day in early August, 1921, in Philadelphia when F. W. Atkins of Jacksonville, Florida, and W. J. Bellang of Cincinnati, Ohio, rented an office in the Bellevue Court Building to quietly recruit members for "A Great and Patriotic Crusade to save the Nation." Their goal was to organize a chapter of the Ku Klux Klan.

When asked by a reporter what the Klan stood for, the response was "Americanism." This meant to protect our women and children, to make the streets safe for women and girls. The various races: yellow, red, black and brown must remain in their place. The Klan accused Catholics of placing allegiance to the Pope above that of their country. The Klan insisted that Jews dominated the banking industry.

The Klan in Pennsylvania

Kleagles (K.K.K. field workers) found recruits in Philadelphia neighborhood row houses. On September 10, 1922, Philadelphia's first outdoor initiation took place in a cornfield on the city's northern border. The burning of a cross twelve feet high and eight feet wide was visible to motorists in the distance. The rally was small compared to the rally in Detroit of twenty-five thousand and Chicago's ten thousand. Nevertheless, a thousand men in white robes standing under American flags watched more than one hundred and twenty-five trembling candidates each paying a fee of ten dollars to take the oath of allegiance. One reporter wrote "Protestant men of mystery, danger and adventure - hooded Knights vowed to protect 'Americanism.'"

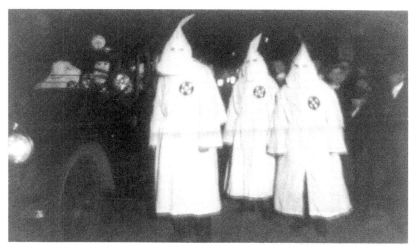

KKK in 1922 parade at height of popularity.

By 1924, Pennsylvania emerged as the most important Klan realm in the Northeast, with two hundred and fifty thousand followers. The Klan was popular in Pennsylvania because it was perceived as a brotherhood with a perfect lodge system. For many, Philadelphia Klaverns were primarily social clubs. Klan members staged late night initiations, gathered for Saturday afternoon picnics, and enjoyed boat excursions on the Delaware River. Unlike elsewhere in the country, the Philadelphia Klan never enjoyed the force of numbers or political power. The city was home to the second largest Catholic population in the nation and large established African-American communities.

When the Klan staged its first organizational rally in July 1924 in quiet and decorous West Chester, a community with a small black and immigrant population, but a good number of Quakers, a crowd of several hundred surrounded Memorial Hall, greeted the Klan with boos and hisses and called out their names to shame them publicly. The K.K.K. gatherings in the counties surrounding Philadelphia often drew crowds who attacked the organization's members.

Surely small groups dropped from the Philadelphia Klan to form smaller ones in their communities, but I have never read or heard of any.

Bonnie Brae Park

******************** REFLECTIONS ****** BY *William C. Brunner*

"The Carousel at Bonnie Brae Park near Spring City"

The Taylor Carousel operated from 1919 to 1925. Pictured in the photo left to right are: Kathryn Snyder Taylor, Clarence Taylor, Caroline Taylor Collopy and Gerald Collopy Sr.

Carousel at Bonnie Brae Park [74]

One group branched off and started their own Klan in northeast Chester County near the town of Spring City, Pennsylvania. In East Pikeland Township abutting East Vincent Township, is where Bonnie Brae Park is located, off Rte 724 between Phoenixville and Spring City. The Park was started about 1899 by the Montgomery and Chester Traction Company to promote summer business.

Horse-drawn carriages at the entrance Bonnie Brae Park between Spring City and Phoenixville Pennsylvania.

The park closed in 1926 and was purchased from Elizabeth Dunmore for $7,500. This consisted of about 25 acres, a penny arcade building which had housed a Merry-Go-Round Carousel, two bungalows, a zoo and a small concession stand. The incorporation certificate was signed by Thomas Todd, Nathan P. Crager, and Horace Hughes.

Bonnie Brae Park Picnic Grove 1910.

The K.K.K. name was never mentioned as the land was named the Bonnie Brae Park Association, Inc. Officers were elected immediately and it was resolved to issue capital stock in the sum of $10,000 having a par value of $5 per share. The Klan tried to pass itself off as sort of a club. They visited Good Shepherd Reformed Church in Boyertown carrying crosses and singing hymns placing a $20 gold piece in the building fund. They visited Sanatoga Union Chapel and other area churches, but despite their contributions, they were greeted everywhere with apprehension.

As soon as funds became available, they added gravel for the roadway, electrical and rest rooms.

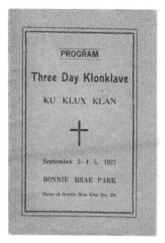

Klan Program

In September, 1927, a three day Klonklave was held which brought Klansmen from near and far at which time the Park was known as the "Home of Bonnie Brae Klan No. 256."

Over the years, other activities at the park included ball games and family reunions and picnics. Early motion pictures were shown in the arcade building using a movie projector, sheet screen and wooden benches. Baseball teams were organized in 1927.

Bonnie Brae Park, Spring City, Pa [75]

A few park events listed included:
• East Vincent Church to hold Festival at the Park ($5.00)
• Locust Grove Home and School League ($5.00), 1928
• Latshaw and Shaner Reunion ($5.00)
• Brownbacks Reunion, 1928.

The K.K.K. presented a flag pole and flag program to the new Spring City High School on June 7, 1929. Horace A. Hughes made the presentation for the K.K.K.

Clipping September 2, 1938 Mercury Newspaper. [76]

After the Ku Klux Klan bought the grounds, they began to hold meetings in the old merry-go-round building. The Klan held services complete with hymnals, singing, and preaching, and crosses were burned to signal meetings and activities. The whole field was covered with horses, wagons and cars.

The 1928 US presidential election rallied the Klan to unite and oppose the election of Alfred Smith, the Democratic candidate for President of the United States. Smith was a Catholic. Rallies were held at the park to oppose his election. Cars were all over the property and roads. Over 2,800 people attended the rally.

In 1924, a historian noted that Klan membership provided the "artificial thrills" which helped relieve the boredom and monotony of small town and rural life. Sometimes,though, such thrills got out of hand.

RESIDENTS MARK LAST HOLIDAY

3000 Expected to Attend Opening of 10th Annual Demonstration Today

The Twin Boroughs are ready to celebrate the last holiday of the Summer with plans made for a busy week-end by those who are going away on trips to the shore, mountains or on extended tours.

Thousands of people will be at home, however, and many visitors were expected with special doings at Lake View park and a big demonstration by Bonnie Brae Klan at Bonnie Brae park near Spring City.

Lake View park will have special attractions both Sunday afternoon and night and Labor Day afternoon and night. The Twin Boroughs baseball club will play at the park Sunday and Labor Day.

The feature attraction at the park Sunday will be Pop Johnson and family, well known radio entertainers from stations WIP and WIBG.

The Texas Rangers, another radio group from WEEU will be at the park Monday afternoon and night.

The 10th annual demonstration by Bonnie Brae Klan at Bonnie Brae park begins today and extends to and including Labor Day. It was expected to attract more than 3000 persons, many of whom will come today and remain at the park the three days, as camping facilities were arranged. Meals will also be available and there is an abundance of parking space.

Mercury September 5, 1936 newspaper
Bonnie Rae Park announcement.[77]

Doctors, lawyers, bank officials, store and land owners, farmers, carpenters and merchants all belonged to the Klan. It was the place to be and belong. There was a lot of disagreement between the Old Guard Democratic party and the new Democratic liberals.

Over the years, the Klan disbanded and the park was sold to a Mr. Shaffy in 1951. Someone had paid the taxes for a number of years.

Chapter 8. Scheib Genealogy

"We all sprang from Adam, therefore, we all have potential for good and evil. There is a strong tendency that those who have little interest whence they come, show little concern from whither they go. Know your ancestors; forgive and avoid their errors; respect and emulate their worthy achievements; and pass on to prosperity a noble heritage that will inspire devotion and loyalty to the highest and best in the human race."
                                        - Anonymous

The lineage charts outline the Scheib ancestors including Brownback, Swinehart and Kubley.

Author Clyde Scheib's grandfather, David Scheib (1836-1919) was born in Germany. The Scheib ancestral village is near Siebenknie, Backnang, Württemberg, Germany. David Scheib came to Pennsylvania after his duty in the Prussian Army.

Clyde Scheib's grandmother is Margueretta Kubley Scheib from Glaris, Switzerland.

The Scheib European ancestry is therefore German and Swiss.[78]

Clyde Scheib Parents

| Walter Scheib
Oct 31, 1895- Dec 1985 | | Gladys S. Swinehart
Aug 31, 1903 - July 1987 |

Clyde Vernon Scheib was born in Birchrunville, Pennsylvania to Walter and Gladys Scheib on November 10, 1925. He married Alda Wenger on May 30, 1948.

Clyde lived his entire life on West Seven Stars Road in East Vincent Township, Pennsylvania. His occupation is "dairy farmer".

Walter Scheib Parents

| David Jasper Scheib Feb 15, 1836 - Jan 30, 1919 | | Margueretta K. Kubley Scheib July 4, 1860-Feb 3, 1952 |

Walter (1895-1985)
Chester David (1886-1958)
Lewis Pinkerton (1889-1976)
Lena Mae Scheib Frame (1893-1985)
Charles (1883-1971)
John J. (1882-1935)
George C. (1899 -1976)

David Jasper Scheib was born in Siebenknie, Backnang, Württemberg. This is current day Germany. The Kingdom of Württemberg existed from 1805 to 1918. David's brothers John (Sept 29, 1822 - Dec 23, 1897) and Charles (Jan 27 1832 - Feb 15, 1917) came to Pennsylvania first, followed by David after his duty in the Prussian Army.

David Scheib lived in Birchrunville, PA and listed occupation was "farmer". He lived to be 82 years old.

Margueretta "Maggie" Kubley Scheib was born in Glarus, Switzerland.

Margueretta or Margareta was married to David J. Scheib on May 27, 1882 when she was 22 years old. David Scheib was 44 years old.

She survived her husband by 33 years. Margueritta Kubley Schieb was 91 years old at the time of her death in Birchrunville, PA.

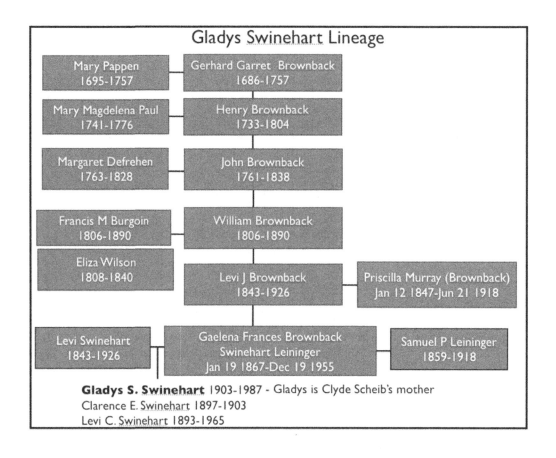

Gladys Swinehart Lineage

Mary Pappen 1695-1757	Gerhard Garret Brownback 1686-1757
Mary Magdelena Paul 1741-1776	Henry Brownback 1733-1804
Margaret Defrehen 1763-1828	John Brownback 1761-1838
Francis M Burgoin 1806-1890	William Brownback 1806-1890
Eliza Wilson 1808-1840	Levi J Brownback 1843-1926

Priscilla Murray (Brownback) Jan 12 1847-Jun 21 1918

| Levi Swinehart 1843-1926 | Gaelena Frances Brownback Swinehart Leininger Jan 19 1867-Dec 19 1955 | Samuel P Leininger 1859-1918 |

Gladys S. Swinehart 1903-1987 - Gladys is Clyde Scheib's mother
Clarence E. Swinehart 1897-1903
Levi C. Swinehart 1893-1965

William Brownback of Chester County Pa
Clyde Scheib's Great Great Grandfather
Levi J. Brownback's Father

William Brownback
1806-1890

The Scheib Brownback Swinehart Connection

Priscilla Murray
Jan 19 1867-Dec 19 1955

Levi Brownback
1843-1926

Gladys S. Swinehart
(baby)1903-1987

Gaelena Frances
Brownback Swinehart
Jan 19 1867-Dec 19 1955

Westley Swinehart
1890-1976

Note: Gladys S. Swinehart (baby) became
Clyde Scheib's mother. She married Walter
Scheib and became Gladys Swinehart Scheib.

From left to right: Priscilla Murray, Levi Brownback, Gladys S.
Swinehart, Gaelena Frances Brownback Swinehart, Westley Swinehart

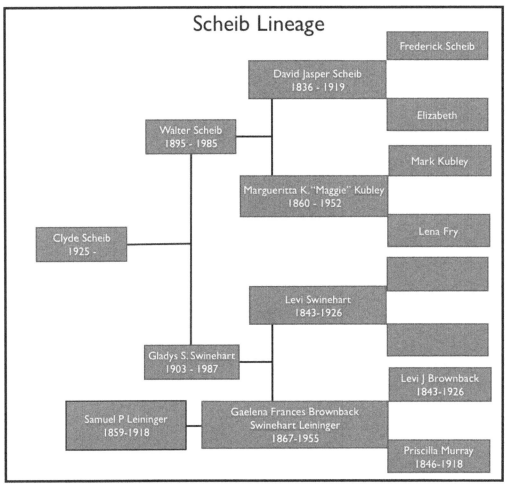

Scheib Lineage

Frederick Scheib

David Jasper Scheib
1836 - 1919

Elizabeth

Walter Scheib
1895 - 1985

Mark Kubley

Margueritta K. "Maggie" Kubley
1860 - 1952

Lena Fry

Clyde Scheib
1925 -

Levi Swinehart
1843-1926

Gladys S. Swinehart
1903 - 1987

Levi J Brownback
1843-1926

Samuel P Leininger
1859-1918

Gaelena Frances Brownback
Swinehart Leininger
1867-1955

Priscilla Murray
1846-1918

Alda Wenger Scheib

Clyde Vernon Scheib

David Jasper Scheib (Feb 15, 1836 - Jan 30, 1919)
David Scheib parents; Frederick Scheib & Elizabeth from Germany. [79]

Margaretta Kubley Scheib (July 4, 1860 - Feb 3, 1952)
Margaretta (Margarita) birthplace as Glarus Switzerland. [80]

Backnang Town Center, Württemberg, Germany. [81]

Backnang is 30 minutes drive NW from Stuttgart Germany

Backnang town center (red dot) in Germany. Backnang is also a district. Upper right is the ancestral village of Siebenknie, where Christina C. Scheib was born on Jan 26, 1822. She is wife of John J. Scheib.

Glarus, Switzerland [82]

Glarus, Switzerland where Margueritta K. "Maggie" Kubley was born on July 4, 1860 to Mark and Lena Fry Kubley. Maggie is Clyde Scheib's grandmother. [83]

Glarus, Switzerland is southwest of Zurich.

Chapter 9. Farming Life

German Heritage

The earliest German settlers followed the rivers to areas populated with black walnut trees. Thriving walnut trees served as barometers of good soil, where we could say, "That was fertile ground".

Because of the densely forested areas, it took at least five years to clear space on which to plant crops. It required the area's earliest farmers to cut down trees, remove stumps and clear rocks from the resulting fields.

The Germans wanted cleared land, but resorted to the crudest of tools and implements to accomplish that end. The Germans made their own implements, utilizing combinations of sticks and rocks as the earliest tools. The axe was the most valuable implement the Germans had, they couldn't cut down a tree with a rifle!

Crude forms of plows emerged as valuable tools, with the earliest ones fashioned from wood. Whatever their minds could devise became an implement for use in some aspect of planting or harvesting.

Those early farmers eventually came to rely on the ingenuity of a blacksmith who had a shop at the time in what is now known as

Knauertown. With his skill and materials he fashioned hoes, shovels and other tools with which the earliest area farmers plied their trade.

Populating local farms with animals was accomplished by bartering, often with farmers from Reading or Lancaster County who brought livestock through the area on the way to market in Philadelphia. Early German farmers sought a male and female pair of cows or attempted to trade an aging animal for a younger one.

The addition of cows and chickens enabled early farmers to provide milk, butter and eggs. The acquisition of horses proved beneficial for heavy labor and eventually to draw wagons and plows.

Such acquisitions were a process. Several transactions from a variety of traders contributed to local farmers' ability to obtain necessary farm animals and implements. It didn't happen in a day.

Prior to about 1840 farmers worked the land they inhabited to grow crops to feed their own families. Everything they grew they ate. As their techniques and tools improved production and output, by the 1840s and 1850s, they grew things to sell. It became commonplace for local farmers to sell grain and butter and to buy or barter for other items from neighbors.

As the population increased, more blacksmiths set up shop throughout the area. There were blacksmiths all over and anything that broke, they fixed it. Blacksmiths used their innovative ideas and craftsman's skills to devise new equipment, particularly in the design of implements that could work the soil. [84]

On my farm in East Vincent Township.[85]

Technology

Technology played a major part in the start-up of local gristmills where grain was milled and sold.

At the time, farmers typically worked 300-acre to 400-acre tracts, selling off portions of land to sons to build their own homesteads and to farm land of their own.

The only way a young man could acquire a farm was to marry into it or inherit. Children on local farms learned farming techniques through early association with the tasks involved. It was common for youngsters to help with milking cows or to help with harvesting crops. The education became an ongoing process in which techniques were passed from one generation to the next.

The main cash crop here was wheat. In the absence of main thoroughfares on which to move goods to market, wheat became a staple to be milled and used locally.

Crude paths and trails were all that offered passage to the "major" roads in the area that included Nutt Road, now Route 23, Conestoga Pike, now Route 401, and Lancaster Pike, now Route 30.

Wheat was the main source of income. Farmers distilled portions of the wheat crop into whiskey. Whiskey always in demand, was used for trade in Philadelphia.

Inventions, resulting from the 19th century's Industrial Revolution, played a significant part in changing both farmers' roles and efficiency. Such innovations as tractors, corn pickers and manure spreaders streamlined farm operations.

As a result of the Great Depression in the early 1930s, 75 percent of farmers lost their farms.

Dairy Operations

In 1941, at 13 years of age, I started farming as a part of my father's dairy operation. I was just a kid and there was a lot to learn and I took advantage of the opportunities to acquire skills and contribute to the work efforts.

As World War II took the supply of farm laborers. Since a lot of farming was manual labor, farmers opted to maintain no more cows than the farmer's wife could milk. With the men absent while dedicated to the war effort, those left to manage dairy operations had to hurry to get milk to its destination to prevent it from going sour.

With farm mowing machine.[86]

The advent of compressors moved the dairy industry forward, enabling milk to be cooled and enhancing its preservation.

Following the war, as I recall, the population boom coupled with technological advances created a bright outlook for farmers. People needed food. Farmers bought more machines to boost production levels.

At the height of my farms dairy operation, I had some 90 cows and some day help. The purchase of tractors and other machinery improved the efficiency of my operation.

After I abandoned the dairy operation, for a time I continued to raise beef cattle and grow hay and corn.

Farming Techniques

Contemporary farming techniques continued to increase production. Technological advancements, improved feed and breeding utilizing artificial insemination all make today's cattle better milk producers. Improvements in livestock management can double the number of livestock on the same land. Advanced farming techniques enable farmers to produce two crops on land where a single crop formerly flourished.

Within the township, less than a handful of dairy farms remain in existence today. In the late 20th century, farmers' offspring got educated and left for better jobs and more money; leaving families on local farms with no heirs and few options in terms of handing down a farm to continue its operation.

Those remaining farms are likely to get a shot in the arm with the open space money.

Meanwhile, those acquainted with agricultural techniques and the labor-intensive efforts required to achieve success in such endeavors have had their ranks continuously reduced.

Those committed to agricultural pursuits are loath to throw in the towel on farming, despite difficulties and obstacles; it "gets in their blood".

Blacksmiths

For early German settlers who sought the fertile soil of East Vincent Township on which to locate their farms, blacksmiths became the earliest tool designers and crafters. Ultimately, numerous blacksmiths populated the area now known as northern Chester County, undertaking the innovative design of implements necessary to clear trees, work the soil and harvest crops.

Discussing farm operations with Barbara Worthington, Pottstown Mercury

In addition to tools, blacksmiths devised such items as hinges and locks. Some blacksmiths had very advanced ideas. Those given to creativity could conjure up innovative gadgets and implements.

Gristmills

Technology played an important part in the capabilities of gristmills which came into existence in the 1840s and 1850s. The use of waterwheels, interlocking gears and crude conveyors enabled grain grown locally to be milled for a variety of uses.

It was also in the 19th century that barbed wire emerged as a boon to confining livestock, creating a method of corralling animals formerly allowed unrestricted open-range grazing.

It was in 1843 that John Deere entered a partnership aimed at development of a steel plow for turning over the soil. The evolution of the steel plow forever altered the face of agriculture.

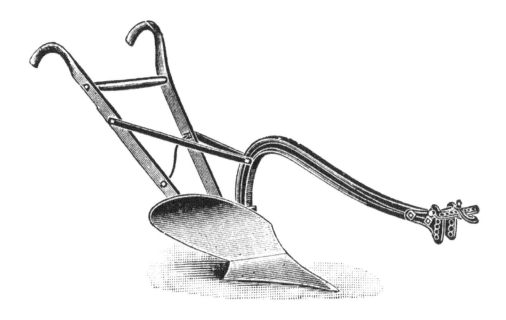

John Deere horse plow that "altered the face of agriculture".

Likewise, Cyrus McCormick's invention of the reaper in the 1850s thrust agricultural pursuits into a new era.

McCormick's invention of the reaper and John Deere's great strides in plow design revolutionized farming as it evolved into the 20th century.

Farmers would go together buying implements, with neighbors frequently pooling their resources to acquire expensive implements and machinery.

The advent of steam-powered tractors and diesel engines spelled the introduction of tractors, corn pickers, hay balers and other farm machinery that streamlined farming operations.

McCormick Reaper

Farmings Future

Dairy farm operations realized a new realm of efficiency with the advent of mechanized milking machines and compressors. Unveiled at the 1915 Panama-Pacific International Exposition in San Francisco, the first mechanized milking machine was introduced by Carnation.

Over the last 90 years, numerous innovations have revolutionized dairy farming as well as agriculture aimed at planting, cultivation, and harvesting of various crops.

Yet because of continuing obstacles, including excessive costs for materials and machinery and operating at the mercy of weather conditions, I fear farming may be a dying skill.

The economics of the situation makes farming a losing proposition. Possibly there will be fewer farms remaining in the township in the future.

Farmings "Way of Life"

People's idea of a farmer is a man with a pitchfork and a wife with a sunbonnet. This is the mistaken notion of farming in the 21st century.

Farming is a business, farmers have taxes to pay. Unlike the open fields with neatly planted rows of crops and rolling countryside and hills many equate with farm life . . . prettiness doesn't pay taxes.

People don't realize what it takes to produce things. For example, consumers, who buy milk, bread, potatoes, carrots, eggs and other farm-generated items, give little thought to what goes into production.

Significant costs are associated with feed for livestock, veterinary bills, fertilizers for various crops, machinery and tools, fuel for machines as well as heat and myriad expenses few consumers stop to consider.

Of increasing concern is the cost of health insurance, paid out-of-pocket by farmers, who are not covered by corporate plans. Gone are the days when a physician could be compensated for delivering a baby with rations of milk and butter or fresh garden vegetables.

The shrinking return for farmers makes agricultural pursuits increasingly difficult. Farmers can't make a living; economics won't let them do it.

The large volume of foods imported from South America at attractive production prices, makes it nearly impossible for American farmers to realize a profit.

Despite the conditions that make farming more and more difficult, it's a way of life and it's a love of the land and the idea of growing things. There's only one thing that can drive a farmer off the land - a nagging wife. [87]

Chapter 10. Two Forgotten Names

This story is about Red Hill and Sheedertown, two forgotten names in East Vincent Township in Chester County, Pennsylvania.

Red Hill Creamery

A group of local farmers established a creamery at the intersection of Pughtown and Sheeder Road. The Red Hill Creamery stood on the southern corner of the intersection. The creamery was built by a cooperative in 1881. They sold stock in the venture for $5 a share and rounded up to $4,000. Unfortunately, the company went bankrupt after a few years and the building was sold at a sheriff's sale.

Red Hill Creamery eventually came into capable hands of Addison Miller who brought the operation back to life. Addison's brother, Clinton, opened a store attached to the milk plant. The Millers also operated Pottstown Creamery. The Millers planned to erect a stone dwelling on the northwest corner of the crossroad. The store burned in 1891, with a loss of everything, including the days mail and $30 worth of stamps. Total damages was estimated at $8,000. Red Hill store reopened after two months. Two years later it burned again, this time by a thief who had robbed the building and then set it on fire.

Ruins of Red Hill Creamery

A Store with a Post Office and Freezer

In 1889, the new Delaware River and Lancaster Railroad (Sowbelly) passed near the store. With the coming of the railroad, a new post office in the store by the name of Sheeder also known as the Vincent Post office was created. The post office closed in 1935. With the coming of the railroad near the store, the Miller brothers bough extra acreage thinking a town would soon spring up. As you can see, to the present day there is no town. Then John Roberts operated the general store and the Vincent Post Office. Roberts built a large house across the road with a Victorian Queen Ann touch. The house remains today. The store closed again in 1936 and was again re-opened by Robert's son M.W. Roberts.

John Robert's House

The back of the store was turned into living quarters. An addition to the front part was made into a grocery store. In the basement, a large freezing unit was installed and space rented for frozen food lockers to quick freeze fruits, vegetables and meat. The period of time was before home freezers were available. This system of preservation was a big advancement in preparing and storing food.

Beside the freezing unit was a meat and vegetable department where you could buy any cuts of meat. The majority of the farmers raised their own livestock for butchering, but brought them to preserve and freeze. In 1945, a large slaughter house was built to process meats for individuals.

This was not successful or profitable. In 1950, the slaughterhouse was leased to S.S. Buckwalter to process turkeys and employed twenty-five employees. The plant was closed and bought by the Arena Beef Company. Problems with sewage and mismanagement of the land finally caused it to close in 1980 and sat as an eyesore to the community. The Green Valleys Association secured the funds and legal works to demolish the building in 1988. The spot was landscaped and allowed a spot to park to fish in the French Creek.

Slaughter Building - an eyesore for the community.

The farmers would bring their eggs and products to trade for groceries. Thirty dozen eggs at $.50 would give you $15.00. Groceries would run you between ten and twelve dollars with three dollars left for pocket money.

In that August in 1904, when John Roberts remarked about Miss Emma Dewees, with a temperamental horse, "Lady" pulling her buggy. On the mail delivery route between Kimberton and Birchrunville, Miss Emma used some pretty strong language to probe the beast. When Miss Emma spoke about dropping the mail at Vincent Post Office, she could not refrain from laughing, noting that in the morning she had a very large leather mail bag and when she turned it upside down to release the mail, only four letters dropped out.

Money Making Farmer

Mr. Roberts makes special note of the farm of Henry Hall. Although Henry had moved away and somebody else bought the place, Henry Hall was known as an industrious and money making farmer. He brought many loads of product to the Kimberton and Phoenixville areas. The covered bridge was named after him until 1990 when the name changed to include Sheeder; the Sheeder-Hall covered bridge stands today.

Sheeder Hall Covered Bridge crosses the French Creek. [88]

Sheeder, Sheedertown or Sheederville

French Creek with its sure and fast supply of water powered many mills. One quarter mile above Red Hill was the Brown Grist water and saw mill. Around the grist mill rose the George David Inn and Sebastian Keely's Inn. Keely bought the Bowen property in 1767 and added a new stone house, located west of the present Sheeder Mill mansion.

Keely kept a store as well as a tavern. Jacob Kelly, son of Sebastian, was a teamster during the revolution, keeping a team constantly gathering forage for the army.

Sebastian Keely House, west of Frederick Sheeder house.

Keely House today, formerly Keely Tavern and Store on first floor.

Conrad Bode Farm

This farm was originally part of he Jacob and Elizabeth Keely tract of 155 acres. In 1827, Conrad Bode bought seventy four acres and operated a tavern until 1830. He sold fourteen acres including the tavern and moved across the new road, Pughtown-Kimberton Road, to the remaining 60 acres and built a new house and barn. In 1892, the property was ordered sold by the courts. Conrad Bode then returned to Germany.

Conrad Bode House

The Local Paper Mill

In 1835. the Bode property came into the possession of Joshua Hause. The sawmill was retained, but the gristmill was torn down and on the foundation, Hause built a paper mill. This was the beginning of the paper business that was bought by Frederick Sheeder and run by the Sheeder family for three generations until 1950.

The Sheeder's made their paper from linen and cotton rags collected over a wide area. Scraps were put aside by every frugal housewife in her rag bag. At times, a rag picker drove his horse and cart up and down Village Street calling out "Raa-a-ags", old rags." This was the signal to bring out the rag bag. The rags were weighed; the ladies were paid a small sum per pound.

When supplies were delivered to the paper mill, the miller used the power of the water wheel to operate a cylinder vessel with revolving knives that shredded, then cleaned and bleached the pulp. The pulp was mixed with clear water and the papermaker stood on a platform at the side of the vat and dipped a mold into the mixture. The mold consisted of a close wire mesh in a removable wooden frame. As the papermaker raised the mold from the vat, a thin layer of pulp adhered to the surface. The excess drained through the wire mesh back into the vat. The screen and frame was removed and the mold was turned upside down on a piece of felt cloth to which the sheet of paper clung. The process was continued to make more sheets until a pile of 144 sheets was collected with felt inserts between each paper sheet. The stack was placed in a massive wooden screw and more water was removed. The sheets of paper were taken to the drying yard and on a sunny day, hung up to dry like towels thrown over a wash line.

Handmade paper was strong and durable and did not discolor with age. The demand for this product was so great that a small operation was able to remain in business for many years.

Ruins of the Sheeder Paper Mill

By the winter of 1845, Sheeder expanded the village of Sheeder by building twenty five houses on his and other farms. This resulted in six families for a total of thirty four people in the village. John W. Dixon was a Manayunk man who built a paper mill one mile north of Sheeder named Dixon Ford. Dixon sank a large amount of money into his mill and started up the operation. A kerosene lamp exploded in the building in January 1871 and caused the place to burn to the ground.

Further north, Cook's Glen Road was named for Sheeder's neighbor, Stephen Cook. Also at the site was Vincent Forge, where the first steel in America was manufactured in 1759 to make axles.

Frederick Sheeder: Historical Writer

In 1845, the Historical Society of Pennsylvania sent out an appeal to the people of the state. The society asked Pennsylvanians to collect and preserve the history of their local regions. One of the few people who responded to the request was Frederick Sheeder of East Vincent Township, Chester County. Sheeder put together a remarkable document on the history of East Vincent Township and surrounding areas. Sheeder went out on horseback from farm to farm to ask people what they knew about their ancestors and properties. In recording this information, Sheeder unintentionally revealed much about himself. Sheeder wrote the history in his second language, English, often writing his sentences without a concern for periods or paragraphs with his grammar sometimes awkward.[89]

Indian Villages

When the German and Welch arrived in Vincent Township, they found the place already occupied. Early records indicate that the land was heavily populated by Lenni-Lenape Indians.

Painting of cave where French Canadian trapper Bezzilian lived.[90]

One of the first Vincent settlers was Joseph Rogers who came over from Ireland about 1712. Rogers settled on the bank of the French Creek, one mile down stream from Sheeder Village, near an Indian village and graves.

Lenape Scene[91]

The Indians lived in wigwams or bank houses. Rogers first lived in an outcropping similar to a cave while he erected his house. He dug a cave in the bank for his slave. Roger's son grew up wrestling and hunting with Indian youths. Another Indian village stood near Sheeder Village when the first white settlers arrived. The Indian dwelt near French Creek in a hollow formed by high banks on three sides with the creek in the front.

A local farmworker and midwife known as "Mother Miller" used to deliver the Indian babies. When she came home she would tell her family how the Indian father would rub the newborn infant with a handful of roots.

Lenape Encampment [92]

Another Indian village once stood in the southern corner of East Vincent at the corner of the two farms. Although the Indians were long gone by the 19th century, the graveyard with twenty-five graves remained. The spot was well known to the locals in 1840. One of the farmers who owned part of the land plowed it over, but that disturbed the spirits resting there. The spot became haunted and the "Indian yell" was heard in the region long after the natives had gone.

The Indians left as a group and migrated westward. One old man did not want to leave. He knew he would not survive the long march. He feared he would fall sick and be left to die on the road. The old man travelled from farm to farm and the white settlers fed him. The old man died during one of his stays with a farmer. David Jenkins, the township supervisor buried him. Jenkins stood alone at the graveside and shoveled dirt on the mortal remains of the lonely Lake Indian of Vincent Township.

Sheeder Mill Farm

Frederick Sheeder was born in the town of Nassau, near the Saarbrucken German region. The family came to Pennsylvania in the spring of 1793. The Sheeder father came to Vincent Township to run a steel mill. Sheeder bought land in Vincent Township in 1799. Years later in 1824, Sheeder built the stone mansion and a large barn and became foreman and paper mill owner.

Sheeder Mill Farm

Sheeder Mill Farm entrance sign.

The West New Jersey Society (Vincent, Thompson and Cox) bought the Chester County land from the Penn family. Since the tenants expected the investors to evict them any day, they lagged behind in improving their land. They did not bother to fertilize and work the fields. Vincent Township got the reputation around Chester County as a township of poor land and farmers.

Sheeder Barn

As the West New Jersey Society sold land back to the tenants after 1793, agriculture took a turn for the better. Farmers began to fertilize and the condition vastly improved. Farms in the region produced high yields of corn, wheat and oats. Other businesses also boomed. Trees yielded to the axe and the whir of the saw mills became a familiar sound.

The date stone reading F.A. Sheeder was 1833. The house was remodeled in 1884 by J. Frederick Sheeder who added a wooden addition and had the chimney rebuilt.

Frederick Sheeder Early Federal style stone house. The Sheeder family lived here for three generations.[93]

Frederick Sheeder was born in 1777 and died in 1865. He and his wife are buried in Zion Lutheran Cemetery on Route 724. The church is located in East Pikeland Township.

Sheeder Mill Bridge

Jacob Keeley's saw mill provided lumber for a small bridge across French Creek giving the public access across the creek when the water was at a high stage. This bridge was strong enough for a horse and buggy. Mother Nature took its course and the wooden boards began to rot and the bridge would collapse or wash away.

Around the Civil War era, a permanent bridge began to appear. An Irish stone mason. John Denithorne, was called upon to build a stronger bridge and laid a stone foundation. Large contracting did not grant small construction. Acquiring columns, straps, strips and bolts, Denithorne constructed the bridge. His firm became known as John Denithorne and Sons. This bridge became known as the Sheeder Mill Bridge.

The bridge which is still in operation allows only one lane of traffic to cross its surface. The iron support of the bridge is high on both sides which is typical of this type of construction. A small oval shaped plaque placed on the support braces which states that it was rebuilt in 1887 by John Denithorne and Sons. The bridge is approximately ninety feet long and sixteen feet wide. It has a posted cross limits of six tons.

#194
Sheeder Mill
Bridge 1887

Sheeder Mill Bridge [94]

In the year of 1958, the Army Corps of Engineers announce the creation of the northern French Creek into a watershed for future use. Plans were for a dam on the French Creek located upstream from Sheeder Village. If the dam would have been built, Pughtown would have been filled with water covering the church and cemetery even reaching as far as Warwick. For some reason, their plans were suddenly halted. Nothing more was ever stated about the project.

Chapter 11. Unknown Soldiers of East Vincent

As the guns fell silent peace came to the little village of Chadds Ford; the Battle of the Brandywine was over. The American Army retreated to the East and the mighty British Army began its march to the rebel capitol of Philadelphia. The War of Independence had come to Chester County.

British Light Infantry and Light Dragoons attacking the Pennsylvania camp September 20, 1777. [95]

Days later, wagon loads of wounded men from the battlefield came up Nutt Road (Rte 23) in search of quarters to house the sick and wounded. Here in this German Reformed Church, they were placed and the war came to the citizens of East Vincent Township.

First German Reformed Church 1758

As the American Army rested at Yellow Springs (in Chester Springs), a local citizen acted as a guide to the Furnaces of Redding and Warwick. This guide lead the troops through Kimberton to the west side of Phoenixville where they crossed a stone bridge over the French Creek. Going there on Route 724 to the Zion Lutheran Church / German Reformed Church which was converted to a hospital. It is reported that the commander of the troops, General George Washington, was a visitor to the hospital/church on more than one occasion.

George Washington outside the Valley Forge Encampment.[96]

As the winter of 1776 approached, more sick was brought from Valley Forge encampment to the German Reformed Church hospital. A great fever broke out and 22 men died. In a mass grave, the men were buried not in the church cemetery but across the street on the farm of Henry Hipple. Hipple put a fence around the graves to protect the site.

East Vincent United Church of Christ. Gothic revival style architecture.

In 1831 a large monument was raised in the cemetery by T.O. Barnard, Nathan Brooke, Captain Worthington and the Battalion of Volunteers of Chester County. Regular military ceremonies were observed and a funeral oration delivered for those that paid the forfeit of their precious lives for our scared rights and privileges which they were never permitted to enjoy. The Appendix has the full inscription on the monument erected.

The following year in 1834, a wall was built around the graves and the monument but with no foundation. In 1926 a roof was built over the monument. Over time, the roof was in disarray and was removed.

Revolutionary Soldiers Cemetery wall in disarray.

The cemetery was maintained by local organizations, but mostly by the Reformed Church. There are no records when the army evacuated the Church.

After the East Vincent Historical Commission was formed, we discovered that no one owned the cemetery. It was recorded but never deeded. The township solicitor and lawyer trusteeship was established by the township so that funds for maintenance and repair of the cemetery could happen.

In 1993, the historical commission began their July 4th Independence Day services, which continue to this day with the Philadelphia Chapter Sons of the American Revolution; American Legion Spring City Post 602 and the Carl Spatz Air Control Guard.

Around this time a new wall was constructed about four feet high. The wall was rebuilt with the help of the Chester County Commissioners and the Department of Housing and Urban development. It was completed and rededicated on July 4, 1997.

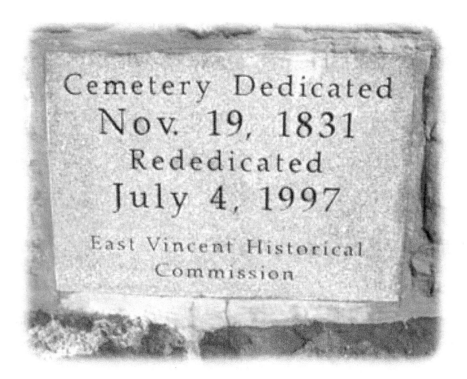

Rededication memorial.[97]

The Church is high on the hill overlooking the entire landscape including the Revolutionary Soldiers Cemetery.

Author at first July 4th, 1994 ceremony.

July 4th, 1995 ceremony.

July 4th, 2019 ceremony. Author at podium.

Historical marker for the Revolutionary Soldiers Cemetery.

July 4, 2019 Ceremony. Procession into the cemetery.

The Philadelphia Chapter Sons of the American Revolution; American Legion Spring City Post 602 and the Carl Spatz Air Control Guard.

This is how The Revolutionary Soldiers Cemetery came to be, across the street from the oldest church in East Vincent Township, known today as the East Vincent United Church of Christ.

Forget them not.

Appendix

I. Scheib Genealogy

In St. Mathews Lutheran Church Cemetery, the tombstone of Christina Scheib (John J. Scheib's wife), shows the exact location where she was born in Germany. This was an important clue as to where in Germany the Scheib family might have lived. The European town is the village of Siebenknie, Baknang, Württemberg. Note the spelling of "Baknang" on the tombstone versus "Backnang" today. Siebenknie is a village in the Backnang district in Bundesland of Baden-Württemberg. This is current day Germany. The Kingdom of Württemberg was a German state that existed from 1805 to 1918. Most likely, the Scheib family in Europe lived in the Backnang district and near the village of Siebenknie.

Christina C. Scheib at St. Mathews Lutheran Church Cemetery,
West Vincent Township, Chester Springs, Pennsylvania

Detail: Christinna C. Scheib wife of John J. Scheib's showing her birth on Jan 26, 1822 as Siebenknie, Backnang, Wurttemberg.

Siebenknie, Backnang, Wurttemberg is probably the Scheib ancestral village. John Scheib's wife Christinna was born in Siebenknie on September 22, 1875. This would require further European research.

Gladys and Walter Scheib in St. Mathews Lutheran Church Cemetery, West Vincent Township, Pennsylvania. Note author Clyde and wife Alda Scheib have placeholders on this tombstone.

Galena Swinehart Leininger (Clyde's grandmother) at Saint Andrew's Cemetery, West Vincent Township, Chester County, Pennsylvania.

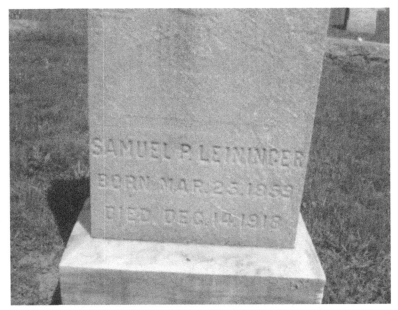

Samuel P. Leininger (Mar 25, 1859- Dec 14, 1918)
Husband to Galena Swinehart Leininger.
Pughtown Baptist Church Cemetery
Pughtown, Chester County, Pennsylvania

Westley Swinehart (Nov 20, 1980 - April 1976)
Brownback's United Church Of Christ Cemetery
Spring City, Chester County, Pennsylvania

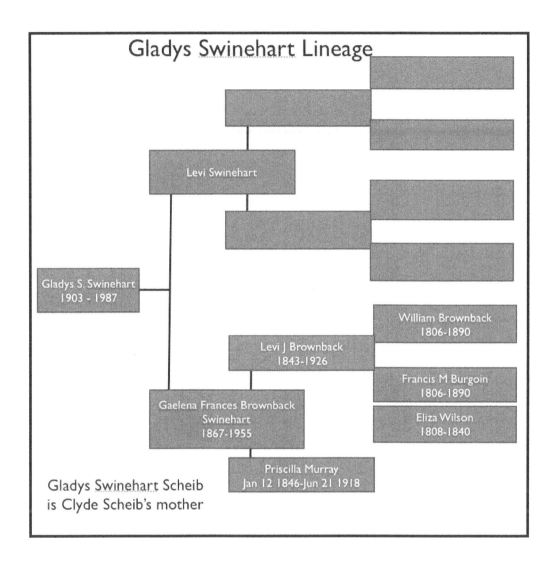

Gladys Swinehart Lineage

Gladys S. Swinehart
1903 - 1987

Levi Swinehart

Gladys Swinehart Scheib
is Clyde Scheib's mother

Gaelena Frances Brownback
Swinehart
1867-1955

Levi J Brownback
1843-1926

William Brownback
1806-1890

Francis M Burgoin
1806-1890

Eliza Wilson
1808-1840

Priscilla Murray
Jan 12 1846-Jun 21 1918

John Swinehart (1817-1893), Mary Swinehart (1820-1903)
St. Mathews Lutheran Church Cemetery, West Vincent Township.

Chester D. Scheib (1886-1958) Walter Scheib's brother.

The Brownback memorial tombstone.
Brownback's United Church Of Christ Cemetery, Spring City, Chester
County, Pennsylvania, USA

The Brownback memorial tombstone.

Priscilla Murray Brownback (Jan 12, 1846 - Jun 21, 1918)
Galena Swinehart's mother; Clyde Scheib's Great Grandmother

Priscilla E. Brownback (Jan 12 1847 - Jun 24 1918)

Note birth year discrepancy tombstone (1847) and death certificate (1846).

Mrs. Levi J. Brownback.

After a lingering illness, Priscilla E., wife of Levi J. Brownback, of Birchrunville, died this morning at her home at 3.15 o'clock. She was seventy-four years of age and a native of that locality, being a daughter of the late Levi and Eliza Murray, of East Nantmeal township. She was a member of St. Matthew's Reformed Church.

Two brothers survive her, Dr. Charles J. I. Murray, of Morris, Ill., and Elmer E. Murray, of East Nantmeal. There are also six daughters: Galena, wife of Samuel Leininger, Birchrunville; Maggie T., wife of Charles Hughes, South Darlington street, West Chester; Lidie, wife of A. H. Kier, California; Mary E. Gilfoy, Philadelphia; Hannah L. Fry, Birchrunville; Anna K. Fulmer, Birchrunville.

About twenty-five grandchildren and six great grandchildren are living.

BROWNBACK.—In Birchrunville, on June 21, 1918, Priscilla E., wife of Levi J. Brownback, in the 74th year of her age.

Relatives and friends are invited to attend the funeral on Tuesday, June 25, 1918, at 2 o'clock p. m. All services at the house. Interment at St. Matthew's Reformed Cemetery. Please omit flowers.

Notes on Brownback (1)

William Brownback was a very successful farmer in Chester Co., PA. He first married Eliza Wilson abt. 1830 and they had four sons and one daughter: Mary, John, James, Wilson, and Lewis Brownback. The last two sons died young. After William Brownback's first wife Eliza died, he married Frances Burgoin about 1842. They had 3 sons and one daughter: Levi, Orlando, Henry, and Galena. Henry and Galena died young. After William Brownback died, Frances Burgoin Brownback left to live with her son Dr. Orlando Brownback and his family in Indiana.

William Brownbach 1806-1890

Henry Brownback married Mary Magdalena Paul abt 1758. They had two daughters and three sons. Henry was the son of Gerhard Brownback and Mary Papen Brownback. At the age of 43, after his children were born, Henry enlisted August 5, 1776 as Ensign in Captain Edward Parker's 2nd Battalion, Chester Militia. He also served in the volunteer militia; light horseman for the company of Chester 1780 to 1781; 2nd Battalion under Colonel Thomas Bull.

On the SAR register of burials, John Brownback married Margaret Defrehn about 1780. They had ten children according to historical accounts. By the time John was 51 years of age, he served as Colonel of the Pennsylvania Militia in the war of 1812.

https://images.findagrave.com/photos250/photos/2012/36/36603365_132855445049.jpg
Scheib message board https://www.ancestry.com/boards/thread.aspx?mv=flat&m=66&p=surnames.scheib

Notes on Brownback (2)

Gerhard "Garrett or Garret" Brownback, according to the "Genealogy of The Brumbach Families" by Gaius Marcus Brumbaugh, pub. 1913, was born in Wertenburg, Saxon, Germany. Information now leads to birth place as Kriegsheim, Alzey-Worms, Rheinland-Pfalz, Germany and to his birth date as 1686 rather than 1682, which was close to his father's birth of 1663. Gerhard Brumbach, Sr. His father died in 1707 in Germantown. His mother was Anaken Liebel Elizabeth Streypp/ Streeper Brumbach. She was born abt. 1657 in Germany and died 1697 in Germantown, just about a year after arrival. Gerhard Garrett Brownback had a sister and brother as well. Heinrich born abt. 1692 died 1759 in what is now Berks, PA.), and Elizabeth who born in the same year as their mother died of 1697. Elizabeth Brumbach married Samuel Oberholtzer. She died in 1759 in North Coventry, Chester County. It has been said that Gerhard immigrated on the Ship Concord from Amsterdam, Netherlands at the age of 21 in September 1683, arriving in Germantown, Pennsylvania Oct. 6, 1683. Much of this incorrect data has been obtained from 'A History of Vincent Township.' Alternative information (source: Estelle Cranmer and Pamela Scheck, "Coventry the Skool Kill District: Basic History of the Three Coventry Townships," pub. 2003), leads us to now believe with accompanying pictures and data that Gerhard arrived with his parents in the port of Philadelphia in 1696. They immigrated with the second wave of Mennonites with Wilhelm Hendricks.

There was only one house that existed when Gerhard and his parents arrived. Gerhard married Mary Papen abt. 1716. Mary Papen's mother was Elizabeth Rittenhouse Papen, daughter of the first paper mill owner in America: Wilhelm Rittenhouse. By 1720 (now shown to be 1736 by Estelle Cranmer), Gerhard had established the Brownback Inn on Nutt's Road. It has been said that General Washington lodged at the Brownback Inn on the night of September 17, 1777 when he marched his troops from Yellow Springs to the furnaces (during the time that Gerhard's son Benjamin owned the inn). We do know that Benjamin served in Captain Edward Parker's Company, 2nd Battalion, Chester Militia, commanded by Colonel Thomas Bull in 1776 and that the inn was frequented by officers and detachments travelling between camps. Gerhard Garret Brownback's Inn was the earliest known inn in Vincent, Chester Co., PA.

Gerhard Brownback donated this property and had the first Vincent Reformed Church built in this area about 1741 so that family, descendants, and neighbors could attend church and be buried here. He also brought the first preacher for this church from Germany: Peter Manicos.

Gerhard Garret Brownback/Brumbach/Brownbaugh's sandstone field stone marker is in this cemetery located near the monument next to his wife's gravestone, Mary Papen Brownback. The markers are not dated.

William Brownbach 1806-1890

https://images.findagrave.com/photos250/photos/2012/36/36603365_132855445049.jpg
Scheib message board https://www.ancestry.com/boards/thread.aspx?mv=flat&m=66&p=surnames.scheib

Brownback Family Storylines

Gerhard Garret Brownback
1686-1757

Gerhard established the Brownback Inn on Nutt's Road, earliest known inn in Vincent Chester County.

Henry Brownback
1733-1804

Henry Brownback married Mary Magdalena Paul abt 1758. They had two daughters and three sons. Henry was the son of Gerhard Brownback and Mary Papen Brownback. At the age of 43, after his children were born, Henry enlisted August 5, 1776 as Ensign in Captain Edward Parker's 2nd Battalion, Chester Militia. He also served in the volunteer militia; light horseman for the company of Chester 1780 to 1781; 2nd Battalion under Colonel Thomas Bull.

John Brownback
1761-1838

John Brownback married Margaret Defrehn about 1780. They had ten children according to historical accounts. By the time John was 51 years of age, he served as Colonel of the Pennsylvania Militia in the war of 1812.

William Brownback
1806-1890

William Brownback was a very successful farmer in Chester Co., PA. He first married Eliza Wilson abt. 1830 and they had four sons and one daughter; Mary, John, James, Wilson, and Lewis Brownback. The last two sons died young. After William Brownback's first wife Eliza died, he married Frances Burgoin about 1842. They had 3 sons and one daughter; Levi, Orlando, Henry, and Galena. Henry and Galena died young. After William Brownback died, Frances Burgoin Brownback left to live with her son Dr. Orlando Brownback and his family in Indiana.

Levi J Brownback
1843-1926

Walter Scheib Lineage

Research fill in blanks

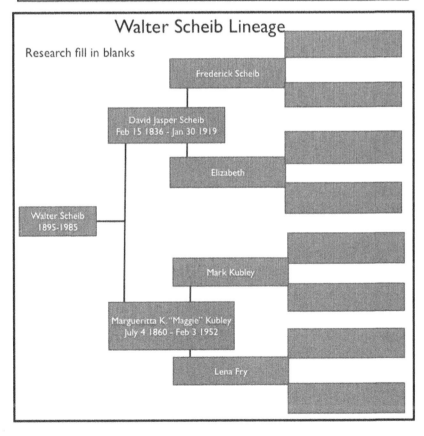

Frederick Scheib

David Jasper Scheib
Feb 15 1836 - Jan 30 1919

Elizabeth

Walter Scheib
1895-1985

Mark Kubley

Margueritta K. "Maggie" Kubley
July 4 1860 - Feb 3 1952

Lena Fry

L7.7.1945

Mrs. Margaret Scheib, of Birchrunville, observed her 85th birthday anniversary on July 4th, and in honor of the occasion a family picnic was held at the home of her son and daughter-in-law, Mr. and Mrs. Walter Scheib, on Kimberton road, East Vincent, on Sunday.

The affair was a surprise to the guest of honor who expected to spend a quiet day at her son's home but did not anticipate a family party. L7.7.1945

Mrs. Scheib was born in Switzerland and came to this country when she was 16 years old. Her husband died 22 years ago. She resides with and keeps house for her son, Louis Scheib. She is one of the oldest members of St. Matthew's Lutheran Church and attended services there Sunday morning.

Those present at the affair included the host, hostess and son, Clyde; Mr. and Mrs. George Scheib, Mr. and Mrs. Harry Huffet and daughter Judy, of Media; Mr. and Mrs. Chester Scheib, Mr. and Mrs. Charles Scheib, and son, Clarence; Mrs. George Scheib and George, Jr.; Louis Scheib, Mr. and Mrs. Bernard Summerfield, all of Birchrunville; Mr. and Mrs. R. Harry Graham, Kimberton; Mr. and Mrs. Nathan White and Miss Sara Ann Shank, Phoenixville.

Mrs. Elwood Fisher, Mrs. John Yearge, Mrs. Furman H. Gyger Jr., Mrs. Harry M. Graham, Mrs. R. Harry Graham, Mrs. Robert Carson, Mrs. Robert E. Funk, Miss Anna Yeager, Mrs. Bernice Heller, Mrs. Beck and Miss Natalie Heller.

Ten members of Kimberton Grange attended the "Traveling Bible" meeting held at Lyndell Grange Monday night, when the Bible was presented by Brandywine Grange. They were Mr. and Mrs. Harry G. Davis, Miss Joan Davis, Mr. and Mrs. Walter P. Cook, Miss Betty May Cook, Furman H. Gyger Jr., Mrs. Furman H. Gyger, Mr. and Mrs. Walter Scheib and Mrs. Myrtle Keen.

Mrs. J. Vernon Styer

DR 7.6.1948

Mrs. Margaret Scheib, Birchrunville, celebrated her 88th birthday anniversary Sunday and in honor of the event a family picnic was held at the home of her son and daughter-in-law, Mr. and Mrs. Walter Scheib, Kimberton road. DR 7.6.48

Dinner and supper were enjoyed and the affair was merry with games and fun.

Attending were Mr. and Mrs. Charles Scheib, Clarence Scheib, Louis Scheib, Mr. and Mrs. George Scheib and George, Jr., Mr. and Mrs. Chester Scheib, Birchrunville; Mr. and Mrs. George Scheib, Mr. and Mrs. Harry Hufford and daughter, Judy, Media; Miss Dorothy Wenger, Schuylkill road; Mr. and Mrs. Harry Fowler, Spring City; Mrs. Nathan P. White and Miss Sara Ann Schenck, Phoenixville; Mrs. Galena Leininger, Mr. and Mrs. Clyde Scheib and Mr. and Mrs. Walter Scheib, the guest of honor and host and hostess.

Mrs. Scheib is in good health and is very active, doing all of her own housework.

DR 7-7-1949

At a family picnic held Sunday at the home of Mr. and Mrs. Walter Scheib and Mr. and Mrs. Clyde Scheib, the Seven Stars-Kimberton road, the 89th birthday anniversary of Walter Scheib's mother, Mrs. Margaret Scheib, of Birchrunville, was celebrated. Dinner and supper were enjoyed at the farm. Her birthday was on July 4th.

Those present included Mr. and Mrs. George Scheib, Mr. and Mrs.

DR 7.26.1947

A family gathering at the home of Mr. and Mrs. Chester Scheib, Birchrunville, marked the 87th birthday anniversary of Mrs. Margaret Scheib, the affair having been postponed until the return home of members of the family. Dinner and supper were served. Mrs. Scheib, the guest of honor, is in fine health and enjoys keeping house. DR 7.26.47

In addition to the host, hostess and guest of honor, those present included: Mrs. Galena Leininger, Mrs. Emma White, Mr. and Mrs. Charles Scheib, Clarence Scheib, Mr. and Mrs. George Scheib, George Scheib Jr. and Louis Scheib, all of Birchrunville; Mr. and Mrs. George Scheib, Mr. and Mrs. Harry Huffet and daughter,

DR 7-7-1949

At a family picnic held Sunday at the home of Mr. and Mrs. Walter Scheib and Mr. and Mrs. Clyde Scheib, the Seven Stars-Kimberton road, the 89th birthday anniversary of Walter Scheib's mother, Mrs. Margaret Scheib, of Birchrunville, was celebrated. Dinner and supper were enjoyed at the farm. Her birthday was on July 4th.

Those present included Mr. and Mrs. George Scheib, Mr. and Mrs. Harry Hufford and daughter, Judy Hufford, and William Arrell, of Media; Mr. and Mrs. Geo. Scheib, George, Jr., and Ruth Ann Scheib, Mr. and Mrs. Charles Scheib, Clarence Scheib, Mrs. Margaret Scheib and Mrs. Chester Scheib, all of Birchrunville; Paul Miller and Mrs. Dorothy Day, of Norristown; Lonnie Day, of Canada; Leon Woodward, of Pocopson; Mrs. Galena Leininger, of Ludwig's Corner; Mrs. Emma White, of Phoenixville; Mr. and Mrs. Harry Fowler, Spring City; Mr. and Mrs. W. Neff Wenger and Miss Dorothy Wenger, Schuylkill road; and Miss Sarah Ann Schenck, Phoenixville, joined the group in the evening.

Margaret Scheib birthday parties (1945,1947,1948,1949) with attendees.

Clyde; Mr. and Mrs. George Scheib, Mr. and Mrs. Harry Huffert and daughter Judy, of Media; Mr. and Mrs. Chester Scheib, Mr. and Mrs. Charles Scheib, and son, Clarence; Mrs. George Scheib and George, Jr.; Louis Scheib. Mr. and Mrs. Bernard Summerfield, all of Birchrunville; Mr. and Mrs. R. Harry Graham, Kimberton; Mr. and Mrs. Nathan White and Miss Sara Ann Shank, Phoenixville.

DR 7.26.1947

A family gathering at the home of Mr. and Mrs. Chester Scheib, Birchrunville, marked the 87th birthday anniversary of Mrs. Margaret Scheib, the affair having been postponed until the return home of members of the family. Dinner and supper were served. Mrs. Scheib, the guest of honor, is in fine health and enjoys keeping house.

DR 7.26.47

In addition to the host, hostess and guest of honor, those present included: Mrs. Galena Leininger, Mrs. Emma White, Mr. and Mrs. Charles Scheib, Clarence Scheib, Mr. and Mrs. George Scheib, George Scheib Jr., and Louis Scheib, all of Birchrunville; Mr. and Mrs. George Scheib, Mr. and Mrs. Harry Huffet and daughter, Judith, all of Media; Mr. and Mrs. Walter Scheib, Clyde Scheib, Miss Alda Wenger, Mr. and Mrs. R. Harry Graham, all of near Kimberton; Miss Nancy Beverly and Miss Sara Ann Schenck, of Birchrunville.

The Young Women's Class of the E. Vincent Church was entertained Monday night at the home of Mr. and Mrs. Paul D. Barton, near Kimberton. Mrs. Barton is teacher of the class and she served a picnic supper. Mrs. Robert Carson was co-hostess.

Mrs. Robert E. Punk presided at the business meeting. A devotional period was conducted by Mrs. Harry M. Graham and Mrs. Frank Taylor. The annual bazaar to be held in October was discussed. Mrs. Merrill Hiltebeitel is general chairman. Subchairmen are: food, Mrs. John Yeager; hand-made articles, Mrs. R. Harry Graham, novelties, Miss Eleanor Gow. It was announced that some of the material has been secured for making the choir gowns and work on this project soon will begin.

A much appreciated letter was read from Mrs. Conant Dodge, now of Tacoma, Washington. It was decided to purchase individual trays to use in serving refreshments at the meetings. Miss Eleanor Gow will be hostess to the class in August.

Those present were the Rev. and Mrs. Robert F. Brillhart, Mrs. Ralph Powell, Mrs. Frank Taylor, Mrs. Boyle Irwin Jr., Miss Ruth Ann Powell, Mrs. Donald Rexrode, the Misses Ruth and Eleanor Gow, Mrs. Wilford Powell, Mrs. Lloyd Mowrer, Mrs. Merrill Hiltebeitel.

---

in honor of the event, a family picnic was held at the home of her son and daughter-in-law, Mr. and Mrs. Walter Scheib, Kimberton road. **DR 7.6.49**

Dinner and supper were enjoyed and the affair was merry with games and fun.

Attending were Mr. and Mrs. Charles Scheib, Clarence Scheib, Louis Scheib, Mr. and Mrs. George Scheib and George, Jr., Mr. and Mrs. Chester Scheib, Birchrunville; Mr. and Mrs. George Scheib, Mr. and Mrs. Harry Hufford and daughter, Judy, Media; Miss Dorothy Wenger, Schuylkill road; Mr. and Mrs. Harry Fowler, Spring City; Mrs. Nathan P. White and Miss Sara Ann Schenck, Phoenixville; Mrs. Galena Leininger, Mr. and Mrs. Clyde Scheib and Mr. and Mrs. Walter Scheib, the guest of honor and host and hostess.

Mrs. Scheib is in good health and is very active, doing all of her own housework.

DR 7-7-1949

At a family picnic held Sunday at the home of Mr. and Mrs. Walter Scheib and Mr. and Mrs. Clyde Scheib, the Seven Stars-Kimberton road, the 89th birthday anniversary of Walter Scheib's mother, Mrs. Margaret Scheib, of Birchrunville, was celebrated. Dinner and supper were enjoyed at the farm. Her birthday was on July 4th.

Those present included: Mr. and Mrs. George Scheib, Mr. and Mrs. Harry Hufford and daughter Judy Hufford, and William Arrell, of Media; Mr. and Mrs. Geo. Scheib, George, Jr., and Ruth Ann Scheib, Mr. and Mrs. Charles Scheib, Clarence Scheib, Mrs. Margaret Scheib and Mrs. Chester Scheib, all of Birchrunville; Paul Miller and Mrs. Dorothy Day, of Norristown; Lennie Day, of Canada; Leon Woodward, of Pocopson; Mrs. Galena Leininger, of Ludwig's Corner; Mrs. Emma White, of Phoenixville; Mr. and Mrs. Harry Fowler, Spring City; Mr. and Mrs. W. Neff Wenger and Miss Dorothy Wenger, Schuylkill road; and Miss Sarah Ann Schenck, Phoenixville, joined the group in the evening.

Scheibe—Veasey 11-12-50

The marriage of Miss Betty Anne Veasey, daughter of Mr. and Mrs. William D. Veasey, of Wilmington, and Max F. Scheibe, Jr., son of Mr. and Mrs. Max F. Scheibe, Sr., of this place, took place in St. Luke's Reformed Episcopal Church, that city, on the evening of Thursday, November 16, with Rev. William Lamming officiating at the ceremony.

IBP 3.7.1952

MRS. MARGUERITTA SCHEIB

Mrs. Margueritta Kubley Scheib, 91, Birchrunville, died at her home Sunday morning at 8, following an illness of two weeks.

Born in Switzerland, Mrs. Scheib came to the United States 76 years ago and lived in Birchrunville since arriving in this country. She was

a member of St. Matthew's Lutheran Church, Ludwig's Corner.

Surviving are 5 sons: Charles, Chester and Lewis, Birchrunville, Walter, Phoenixville, R. D., and George, Media; 16 grandchildren and seven great-grandchildren. Her husband died over 20 years ago.

Services were held in the Nelson Funeral Home, 331 New Street, Spring City this afternoon at 2. Interment followed in St. Matthew's Lutheran cemetery.

Margueritta Scheib

II. The Village Name Controversy

There are multiple names for the village of Parkerford, Pennsylvania: "Parkerford", one word, "Parker Ford" (two words) and "Olde Parkerford".

For our walking tour we used the name, "Olde Parkerford", which was the alternate name of the village.

In Washington's letter written in 1777 from the immediate area, he used "Parker's Ford".

There are many historic photos of this area which use the spelling as one word; "Parkerford". A sign on the Route 724 uses the name Parkerford, as well. *The Master Plan for the Parkerford Tavern March 2005* uses the one word version; "Parkerford".

Yet, the official name at the Post Office is listed as two words; "Parker Ford". Also, the Google maps and Apple maps use "Parker Ford" two words as well. Many in East Coventry Township use the "Parker Ford" name as does the Post Office.

The meaning behind the name is:
• "Parker" referencing Edward Parker
• Ford, referencing the shallow water crossed by foot or horse and carriage. The ford bottom can be silt, rocks or sand.

For this document, I have used what I believe is the correct spelling: "Parker Ford" two words. For the tavern, I use Parker's Tavern.

III. Oral History

A Day at the One Room Schoolhouse - Irma Eppehimer Wall (2004)[98]
School started at 8:00 in the morning. We finished by 4:00 p.m. It was a typical one-room school. I remember that there were little chairs up on the platform. When it was our turn for a subject, we would go up front and sit on those chairs. The teacher would take each grade up front and they would have their lesson up there. Penmanship was emphasized.

In school, we had plenty of time to do our homework while other classes were in session. We always had penmanship. The last class on Friday afternoon was penmanship. That was where I really learned to write.

My classmates names were John Hallman, Raymond Wentzel, Elsie Law, Betty Finkbiner and James Lockart. I went through all eight grades with these classmates.

Russel Latshaw was the school director over several schools. He would have had Bertolet, Hickory Grove, Salem, Mt. Pleasant and Locust Grove.

The one room school house, Bertolet School (on Pughtown Road) was at least a mile and a half for me to walk. That was a bit of a trudge in the snow. There were no school buses. My Dad used to ship milk to Sunny Slope Dairy in cans. So I used to ride along in the morning when they were taking milk to Sunny Slope to Heistands Store, also called the Red Rooster for a while.

The high school nurse used to come across from Glenmoore. She used to pick me up at Heistand's Store and take me to high school. Then at night, she would drop me off at Brownbacks Church on Rte 23 and I had to walk home down Brownbacks Church Road. That was a good mile.

The teacher taught all eight grades. There was no plumbing at the school. We had to carry water by the bucket from the Fischer house on Pughtown Road and the Potts house on Bertolet Road. There was a large heater in the corner of the school that was fired by coal. The boys had to carry the coal up from the basement of the school to the fire heater.

Boys and girls played together at Bertolet School. The main thing was baseball. I am a fan of baseball, especially a fan of the Phillies.

Probably my teachers were the greatest influence on me. I think my grade school teacher that taught us was an influence. We were in a small group and I think I really learned more there than when I went to high school. In high school, we had to change teachers every class. We had lockers and we had to change for every subject. Up to ninth grade, the teachers were almost like part of the family because of the close relationships. I would not have wanted to change anything about that. I did make it through Spring City High School graduating in 1946. They have high school reunions but I don't attend.

Seven Stars Inn - Irma Eppehimer Wall (from 2004)[99]
I remember Seven Stars as a restaurant. I used to go there on my lunch hour from Sunny Slope and get lunch there. Sunny Slope was where Parmalot is now. Inside was a counter and tables. It was mostly just the first floor then. Girls would board there and work in the store.

Farming Life - Irma Eppehimer Wall (from 2004)[100]
My Dad had a few pigs and twenty five dairy cattle. He bred his own cattle. The bull had a special place in the barn. That was his stall. He did not go out to pasture. I usually stayed away from him (the bull).

My Dad used to sell pigs, but then he would butcher a pig for our own use.

When I was on the farm, we did a lot of picking vegetables. My mother and I used to can and then later we froze vegetables. It was mostly just a farm for the family. We didn't go the market with the vegetables.

The farmer of yesterday did truly hard labor. If they did go to market, the wife was working right there with him.

It was always a big thing to get your silo filled. There were at least five farmers that would get together. There names were: Clarence Shantz, Earl Law, Paul Keely, Jack Hewitt (father of Robert Hewitt), George Brownback and then my Dad. The six farmers worked together and then they rotated and helped each other. They cut corn by hand. They went through row by row, cut the corn and laid it in piles. Then it had to be put on wagons. Then it was taken to the silos by horse and wagons. So they gave each one a day until they got their silos filled. It would take a day for each one.

We used to store our potatoes in the cold cellar for the winter. That was always a big job to get the potatoes picked and put in the cellar. This was common practice. Without a cellar, a family was in trouble.

A man who had an egg rout in Phoenixville, would come every Wednesday night to pick up the eggs. I remember helping him pack the eggs in egg crates; the old wooden frame ones.

Seven Stars Inn - Donald Overdorf Francis (2004)[101]
Seven Stars was a soda bar and restaurant for many years before they got their liquor license (1960/70). They were a family restaurant and soda fountain with a juke box. My wife worked there... a lot of waitresses stayed there overnight. They weren't allowed to take their dates in the hotel. Russel Latshaw, the owner of the hotel, was very strict about that.

Indian Settlement - Donald Overdorf Francis (2004)[102]
There was a very large Indian settlement up near Brownback Church. The Schuylkill River is a haven for finding Indian relics. I know people in Spring City and Royersford that have collections of thousands of arrowheads that have been found just along the Schuylkill River banks.

There is an Indian burial ground located on Pennhurst property. There are still people living today that can pinpoint it. Marian Fry Ferrara was an honorary tribal member up in New york, but she passed away. Basically everything I hear about the Indian burial ground is heresy, yet most of the older people in the area are very much aware of it.

Farming Life - Phyllis Powell (2004)[103]
East Vincent has boasted many well kept dairy farms. Bridge Street farms were Latschar, Simon & Mourer. They all produced enough milk to service the surrounding area. Simon Dairy was the first to discontinue milk delivery. Our family was then served by Maurer Dairy. When my children were born, Joe Latschar was our milk supply person. He came in a white wagon drawn by a very patient horse. Joe's horse would walk slowly as Joe advanced along his route. The horse knew where to stop without any real verbal instructions.

Parker's Tavern - Richard "Dick" Mull (2006)[104]
My Dad lived right along what was then the canal, you know the Schuylkill Canal at Parker Ford, that was used when he was a little kid. He saw the donkeys pulling the barges and that whole bit. They swam in the canal all the time. Yes, that was their swimming pool at that time.

The young guys used to have their horse and buggy and they would race up and down the road, it was a dirt road. Old Schuylkill Road was a dirt road. That was their entertainment. You've got to remember there was no television back then. In my father's younger days, there wasn't even a radio.

When East Vincent started talking about the tavern, I wanted to find out if anybody heard of it.

All you ever heard about down there (Parker Ford), where it was Murray's Row and "stay out of there!" You don't go down there because you'll get in trouble. Because I guess in the depression, the poorest of the poor must have lived down there ... lived in all those old houses down there. (now torn down). We weren't suppose to go down there. But I asked the oldest people that lived down there, like the Malenkes (they had a bakery with fresh bread and sticky buns) and all the people I knew who grew up there, like the Willaurs, "Did you ever hear of George Washington being down in Parker Ford?" Well they never heard of Parker's Tavern nor of George Washington being there. We knew that he was supposed to have slept down at the South Inn, in that building. He was suppose to have been there and of course, down in Valley Forge.

IV. East Vincent's Unknown Soldiers

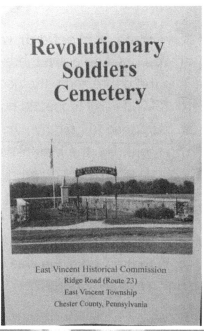

Revolutionary Soldiers Cemetery with Monument.

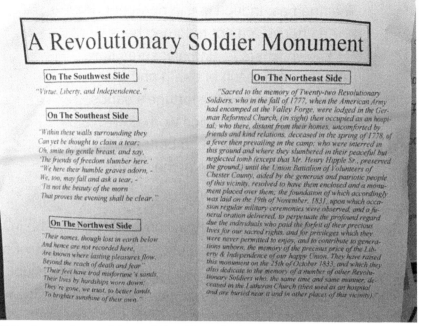

Tribute on four sides of the Revolutionary Soldiers Monument.

On The Southwest Side:

Virtue, Liberty, and Independence.

On The Southeast Side:

Within these walls surrounding they
Can yet be thought to claim a tear;
Oh, smite thy gentle breast, and say,
The friends of freedom slumber here.
We here their humble graves adorn,
We, too, mayfall and ask a tear,
'Tis not the beauty of the morn
That proves the evening shall be clear.

On The Northwest Side:
Their names, though lost in earth below
And hence are not recorded here,
Are known where lasting pleasures flow,
Beyond the reach of death and fear
Their feet have trod misfortune's sands,
Their lives by hardships worn down;
They're gone, we trust, to better lands,
To brighter sunshine of their own.

On The Northeast Side:

Sacred to the memory of Twenty-two Revolutionary Soldiers, who in the fall of 1777, when the American Army had encamped at the Valley Forge, were lodged in the German Reformed Church, (in sight) then occupied as a hospital; who there, distant from their homes, uncomforted by friends and kind relations, deceased in the spring of 1778, of a fever then prevailing in the camp; who were interred in this ground and where they slumbered in their peaceful but neglected tomb (except that Mr. Henry Hipple Sr., preserved the ground,) until the Union Battalion of Volunteers of Chester County, aided by the generous and patriotic people of this vicinity, resolved to have them enclosed and a monument placed over them; the foundation of which accordingly was laid on the l9th of November, 1831, upon which occasion regular military ceremonies were observed, and a funeral oration delivered, to perpetuate the profound regard due the individuals who paid the forfeit of their precious lives for our sacred rights, and for privileges which they were never permitted to enjoy, and to contribute to generations unborn, the memory of the precious price of the Liberty & Independence of our happy Union. They have raised this monument on the 25th of October 1833, and which they also dedicate to the memory of a number of other Revolutionary Soldiers who, the same time and same manner, deceased in the Lutheran Church (then used as an hospital and are buried near it and in other places of this vicinity).

Author as Master of Ceremony with East Vincent Township Vice
Chairman Ed Dracup on July 4th, 2019.
A crowd of 75 citizens were in attendance.

East Vincent Township (Pa) Supervisor Jane Peronteau and Vice
Chairman Ed Dracup at attention in front of flag
during July 4th, 2019 Independence Day Ceremony.

Route 23 was closed for the July 4th 2019 Independence Day Ceremony.

German Reformed Church

Background on the German Reformed Church

"About the same time, a Lutheran pastor arrived to care for those of that tradition. Both congregations, the German Reformed and the Zion Lutherans, shared the same facility and grew as the population increased. Before long, the building proved to be too small to serve both congregations comfortably. The difficulty was solved by the separation of the two congregations. The Lutherans continued in the building with a name that is still with us today, Zion Lutheran. The Reformed Congregation surrendered their rights and established a separate fellowship. They erected a new log cabin church about one mile to the south of the original one. It was dedicated on May 27, 1758, with John Philip Leydich continuing to serve as the first pastor."

- Dr. Robert W. Price[105]

"Eventually. the roof over the monument was removed and the wall came into disrepair. An eight-year project was undertaken by the newly formed East Vincent Historical Commission to rebuild the wall. Since the wall had no foundation and was structurally unsound, the entire wall was demolished. The new wall began with construction of a foundation and was built about four feet high. The wall was rebuilt with the help of the Chester County Commissioners and the Department of Housing and Urban development. It was completed and rededicated on July 4, 1997."
- Dr. Robert W. Price[106]

German Reformed Church marker.

German Reformed Church marker.

"The oldest church in our township, the one that can trace its roots all the way back to 1733, was officially organized as the German Reformed Congregation and gained its first pastor about 1750. Their first church building after separating from Zion Lutheran was a log cabin erected in 1756. Those early members were just getting off to a good start when the political troubles began to grow that eventually brought on the War of Independence from the British in 1775 & 1776."

- Dr. Robert W. Price[107]

Church marker.

United Church of Christ / East Vincent Church

East Vincent United Church of Christ.

Stone marker (1779). Buggy sheds on the right.

V. Covered Bridge Society

The Theodore Burr Covered Bridge Society of Pennsylvania is a non profit organization that promotes interest and active participation in the preservation and restoration of the remaining historic covered bridges in the Commonwealth of Pennsylvania. Clyde Scheib has been an active member of this society.

A magazine, *Wooden Covered Spans,* is issued once a year. A newsletter, *Pennsylvania Crossings,* is issued three times a year in a black and white hard copy version and an electronic color edition. Publications are not available without membership.

The Theodore Burr Covered Bridge Society of PA is a 501(c)(3) Nonprofit Public Charity Organization

A COLLECTION OF NEWS ITEMS, REPORTS AND ANNOUNCEMENTS FOR FALL 2017 (VOL. 41, NO. 1)

FEATURE BRIDGE – Kurtz's Mill Bridge in Lancaster County, PA.
Built in 1876, Kurtz's Mill Bridge was lifted from its abutments during Tropical Storm Agnes in June of 1972. The bridge was rebuilt saving most of its original trusses and moved to Lancaster County Park over Mill Creek.   *Photo by Bob Howden*

Covered Bridge Society Newsletter

VI. Community Activities of Author (Clyde Scheib)

*"**A community is like a ship; everyone ought to be prepared to take the helm.**"* - Henrik Ibsen 1882 [108]

I am a charter member of the East Vincent Township Historical Commission.

While at the commission I was involved in:

- rebuilding of the Kennedy Bridge after the fire burned it down;
- restoration of the Old Hickory Grove School;
- Revolutionary Soldiers Cemetery;
- coordinator of the annual July 4th Cemetery;
- Friends of the Kennedy Covered Bridge
- annual Christmas luminaries at the Kennedy Bridge; and
- purchase of the historic Parkerford Tavern.

I'm in the 70th year as a member of the Kimberton Grange #1304 at the county, state and national levels.

VII. Kennedy Covered Bridge Fire and Restoration

Evening Phoenix May 10, 1986

Newspaper account of the fire at the Kennedy Covered Bridge. Blaze started at 5:24 a.m. Sixty firefighters from Ridge and Kimberton fire companies fought blaze at each end of bridge. Chief Robert Dobson of Kimberton Fire Company said blaze was put out in half an hour with no injuries.

5,000 sign petition to restore bridge

By E.J. BROWN
Staff Writer

More than 5,000 people have signed petitions saying they want the historic Kennedy Covered Bridge in East Vincent Township fully restored, according to an advocate of the project.

Clyde Scheib, chairman of a committee working for restoration of the bridge, announced the signature totals recently, and said the petitions will be sent to the Chester County Commissioners.

The 130-year-old bridge was destroyed in a fire May 10. A public meeting to discuss the project is scheduled at 8 p.m. on Monday at the Kimberton Waldorf School on West Seven Stars Road, Kimberton, where petitions will be collected.

"We want to begin compiling them for the Sept. 23 meeting when we will present them to the county commissioners. Also, we want people to take more blank petitions and get as many new signatures as possible," he said.

A representative of the Theodore Burr Covered Bridge Society will be at the meeting to discuss the historical and architectural significance of covered bridges.

The wooden bridge was reduced to a skeleton in the blaze four months ago. Only the steel beams and trusses remained intact. The fire was labeled suspicious in origin by the Chester County Fire Marshall.

The petition drive, begun in July, was spearheaded by the Committee to Restore the Kennedy Covered Bridge, which established a $700 reward for anyone who could provide information leading to the conviction of the person or persons responsible for the fire.

County engineers have built a temporary timber deck bridge to handle traffic since the fire. Rich Craig, a Chester County bridge engineer, told the committee in August that the temporary structure is only meant to last one or two years.

A feasibility study on the type of permanent structure that would best replace the bridge is currently being

(See BRIDGE, P2)

• Bridge

(Continued from Page 1)

undertaken, and is expected to be completed by November.

Both state Rep. Samuel Morris (D-155) and his Republican opponent in the upcoming state elections, J. Barry Pignoli, spoke in favor of the a restoration project at a bridge committee meeting in July.

Efforts of the Kennedy Bridge Restoration Committee
Evening Phoenix September 6, 1986

Staff photos by Liz Andrews Willow

Invited dignitaries are driven across the new Kennedy Covered Bridge in antique cars during ceremonies Wed.

Historic dedication to a covered bridge

By KONRAD SUROWIEC
Evening Phoenix Staff

EAST VINCENT — Dairy farmer Clyde Scheib says it was worth every penny to rebuild the Kennedy Covered Bridge. It serves a purpose, he says, and it preserves a part of an era gone by at the same time.

Scheib was among more than 50 area residents and municipal and county officials at the dedication ceremony Wednesday to celebrate the reopening of the historic bridge. The bridge crosses the French Creek on West Seven Stars Road in East Vincent Township.

Scheib, a lifelong township resident, operates his farm just west of the bridge. He led the Kennedy Bridge Restoration Committee in the effort to have a bridge recovered after it was destroyed by a fire more than two years ago.

"We, the citizens, wanted the bridge rebuilt," Scheib said, speaking after the dedication. "We wanted to pre-

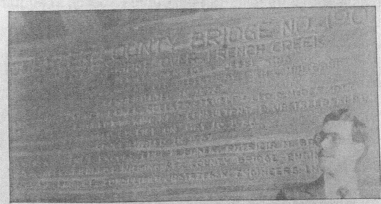

Richard Craig was instrumental in carrying out the rebuilding project

serve the rural integrity of the area. To build a horse-and-buggy bridge, we were asking to come back in time instead of forward. I enjoy it, and I'm glad to restore it."

Chester County Commissioners' Chairwoman Irene Brooks praised the committee for gathering more than 5,000 signatures on a petition presented to her board.

The original bridge was built in 1856 by Alexander Kennedy and Jesse King for $2,149. It was rededicated in 1978 after it

(See BRIDGE, P2)

Evening Phoenix - Dignitaries drove in vintage cars across the Kennedy Covered Bridge during dedication ceremony.

VIII. Kimberton Grange #1304

Local Kimberton Grange #1304 is a family-oriented fraternal organization dedicated to the betterment of rural Pennsylvania through community service, education, legislation and fellowship. The National Grange (the Order of Patrons of Husbandry) had been established in 1867 with the objectives of promoting cooperative purchasing, lowering of railroad rates, and rural free delivery. The author is a long time member of this organization at the local and national levels.

The Granges pioneered the movement to give equal status to women. Headquartered at 20 Erford Road, Lemoyne, Pennsylvania, this grassroots organization continues to be "the voice for rural Pennsylvania."

Grange Motto:
"In essentials unity, in non-essentials liberty, in all things charity."

PA State Grange shared a link.
October 30 at 7:38 AM ·

MORNINGAGCLIPS.COM
New tool released to calculate value of Pa. dairy
HARRISBURG, Pa. -- With statewide dairy production and associated...

Pennsylvania Grange Facebook Page

Bibliography

Cremers, Estelle *30,000 Acres, Vincent and Pikeland Townships 1686 to 1850* (1989)

Lockart, James *Sowbelly RR The Delaware River and Lancaster Railroad* (2008)

East Vincent Township 175 Years 1832-2007

Sheeder, Frederick, *East Vincent Township, Chester County, Pennsylvania* (1846)

Futhey, John and Cope, Gilbert (1881). *History of Chester County, Pennsylvania, with genealogical and biographical sketches. Philadelphia: L. H. Everts.*

Sowbelly RR The Delaware River and Lancaster Railroad by James Lockart

Acknowledgments

Several people and organizations impacted my knowledge of the local history.

Carl McIlroy was the first Chairman of the East Vincent Township Historical Commission and was instrumental in getting the Revolutionary Soldiers Cemetery set up. He used to walk by the cemetery noting it's disrepair until one day he decided to take action and we are all better for it. Carl was the type that just got things done. He was the captain and I was the lieutenant.

Estelle Cremers was a dear friend and neighbor with her family's farm on West Seven Stars Road. I helped with her book, *30,000 Acres Vincent and Pikeland Townships 1686 to 1850.* She was detail oriented and when she had a question she would call me multiple times over several days to get a full understanding from me. She always told me, "Save that tavern" referencing Parker's Tavern in Parker Ford, Pennsylvania. She and her husband William Cremers later sold their farm and moved to another area.

Alda Scheib is my severest critic and my wife of over 70 years. Her diligence has kept me on track. We have attended many local community events and talks together and she is always there to add to the conversation.

Kimberton Grange is a farmers association of men and women that I was asked to join in 1942. They are a wealth of information and I respect this organization highly. They are patrons of husbandry and started the rural free delivery (mail) program.

The nearby historical societies have provided knowledgeable speakers and their expertise have further expanded my knowledge base. These include the Limerick Township Historical Society, Historical Society of the Phoenixville Area, East Vincent Township Historical Commission, Spring-Ford Area Historical Society and the Pikeland Historical Society.

East Vincent Township has been a part of my life and I have enjoyed contributing to the Historical Commission as Chairman and Chairman Emeritus. I have been Master of Ceremonies for the July 4th ceremony at our Revolutionary Soldiers Cemetery and each year Mary Flagg, the township manager, has helped me plan the ceremony and many other functions for which I am thankful.

The Theodore Covered Bridge Society of PA have shared their expertise on covered bridges. I have made numerous outings with this group to discover covered bridge design and history in Pennsylvania.

My neighbor, Brian Wilde, absorbed the local history and together we met regularly as friends to discuss my history stories. He documented and published this book and we had a lot of fun along the way.

Endnotes

Chapters 1-11 and Appendix

[1] Kimberton Village with Boarding School circa 1835 by John Pierce

[2] Inventory of Church Archives: Society of Friends in Pennsylvania

[3] 30,000 Acres Vincent and Pikeland Townships 1686 to 1850 by Estelle Cremers

[4] Ibid.

[5] Ibid.

[6] Clyde Scheib personal files

[7] The Old Kennedy Place from Mr. Bridgr. View from Kennedy Covered Bridge with Kennedy House on right and barn on left.

[8] East Vincent Township - Rededication of the Kennedy Bridge flier

[9] Brunner, William Spring Ford Area Historical Society

[10] The Desecration and Profanation of the PA Capitol. 1911

[11] The Kimberton Waldorf School

[12] Ibid.

[13] Beras International

[14] Aberdeen-Angus Cattle Society

[15] Seven Stars Yogurt Farm Facebook

[16] The Kimberton Waldorf School

[17] Morning Verse of the Upper School, Kimberton Farms School, Dedication of the New Upper School. Oct 8, 1964

[18] Photo: Harvest Market Natural Foods.

[19] Source: Seven Stars Yogurt Farm Facebook Page

[20] Ibid.

[21] Kimberton Whole Foods

[22] Source: Seven Stars Yogurt Farm

23 Photo courtesy of Kimberton CSA

24 Photo courtesy of Kimberton CSA

25 Annals of Phoenixville and its Vicinity. From the Settlement to the Year 1874, by Samuel Pennypacker. Page 72.

26 Photo from *Reading Furnace 1736*, by Estelle Cremers, back inside cover

27 From Seven Stars Inn web site

28 East Vincent Township Master Plan Parkerford Tavern circa 2005

29 East Vincent Township Historical Commission - township web site

30 East Vincent Township Master Plan Parkerford Tavern circa 2005

31 Parker's Tavern: It's Place in History The Story of George Washington's Ride to the Schuylkill by Clyde Scheib

32 The Hill School, Pottstown, PA; photographed by C.F. Gachet

33 The Hill School, Pottstown, PA; photographed by C.C.F. Gachet Washington at Valley Forge, by Pennsylvania artist N.C. Wyeth, is in the collection of the Hill School in Pottstown, PA

34 Limerick History by Muriel E. Lichenwalner

35 Mordecai Evans house photo Brian Wilde

36 Spring - Ford Area Historical Society Facebook

37 Parker Ford, National Register of Historic Places 1982

38 Post cards courtesy Rosemarie C. Miller and Glen A. Miller

39 The East Vincent Township Historical Commission organized and conducted this tour of Parker Ford Village in 1996

40 Spring - Ford Area Historical Society Facebook

41 Source: "History of the Schuylkill Navigation System" Reading Area Community College

42 East of the wye is a bridge crossing over Mine Run Stream. Neil Brennen photo

43 Source: Abandoned Rails.com
http://www.abandonedrails.com/Delaware_River_and_Lancaster_Railroad

[44] Painting French Creek Falls Station by Linda R. Killingsworth from *Sowbelly RR The Delaware River and Lancaster Railroad* by James Lockart 2008

[45] The Delaware River and Lancaster Railroad French Creek Branch (Sowbelly Railroad) Official Guide Booklet December 1, 1890.

[46] Penn Pilot

[47] Clyde Scheib personal collection

[48] Penn Pilot

[49] LivingPlaces.com Chester County Coventryville Historic District

[50] Penn Pilot

[51] Ibid.

[52] Chester County Historical Society; Phoenixville Historical Society; John Noble, deceased; John V. Norris, 1973 personal account in the Daily Republican; Russell Amalong; original typing; Estelle Cremers, editing and suggestions

[53] Ibid.

[54] Cal Roth Collection

[55] Penn Pilot

[56] Cal Roth Collection

[57] Chester County Historical Society

[58] Interview by Patty Moore. "Oral History with Clyde Scheib" 2010. Audio recording with transcripts. Modified.

[59] George Washington painting by John Trumball

[60] Wikipedia

[61] Interview by Patty Moore. "Oral History with Clyde Scheib" 2010

[62] History of the Underground Railroad in Chester County by R.C. Smedley M.D. 1883 West Chester PA

[63] Cremers, Estelle 30,000 Acres Pikeland and Vincent Townships 1686-1850

[64] Fugitive slaves fleeing the Maryland coast 1850 Peter Newark Bridgeman Images

[65] National Geographic wiki

[66] History of the Underground Railroad in Chester County by R.C. Smedley M.D. 1883 West Chester PA

[67] Ibid.

[68] Ibid.

[69] Ibid.

[70] Ibid

[71] Ibid

[72] Ibid

[73] Futhey, John and Cope, Gilbert (1881). History of Chester County, Pennsylvania, with genealogical and biographical sketches. Philadelphia: L. H. Everts.

[74] Spring Ford Area Historical Society - Courtesy of William Brunner

[75] Published by The St. Clair Card Company, Royersford, Pa

[76] Clyde Scheib materials

[77] Heritage Magazine, Fall 2002
Charles Hardy III, Professor of History, West Chester University

[78] Ancestry.com

[79] Find a Grave website, Scheib family at St. Matthews Lutheran Church, Chester Springs PA

[80] Ibid.

[81] Backnang Town Center, Württemberg, Germany Wikipedia

[82] Glaris Switzerland Wikipedia

[83] Ibid.

[84] Adapted from Barbara Worthington interview of Clyde Scheib, Pottstown Mercury Newspaper, Pottsmerc.com, Aug 2, 2004.

[85] Ibid.

[86] Ibid.

[87] Ibid.

[88] Wikipedia

[89] *East Vincent Township, Chester County Pennsylvania* by Frederick Sheeder 1846

[90] Bezaillion Print by Dorothy S. Weikel

[91] Legends of America: Lenape Delaware Tribe

[92] Ibid.

[93] High Priority Resources as per Chester County Architecture / Historic Resources Survey 1982

[94] East Vincent Township Historical Commission.

[95] Xavier della Gatta painting 1782

[96] Washington and Lafayette at Valley Forge December 19, 1777 – June 19, 1778 by John Ward Dunsmore 1907

[97] East Vincent Township Historical Commission

[98] Wall, Irma Pauline Eppeihimer: Oral History: Her Life in East Vincent Township. Interviewed by Dr. Elaine Husted, East Vincent Township Historical Commission, March 29, 2004.

[99] Ibid.

[100] Ibid.

[101] Donald Overdorf Francis, Oral History, Interviewed by Dr. Elaine Husted, East Vincent Township Historical Commission, May 26, 2004

[102] Ibid.

[103] Powell, Phyllis: Oral History, Interviewed by Dr. Elaine Husted, East Vincent Township Historical Commission, January, 2004

[104] Mull, Richard (Dick) Lewis: Oral History, Interviewed by Dr. Elaine Husted April 10, 2006

[105] Price, Dr. Robert W., East Vincent Township Historical Commission, East Vincent Township, Pa website

[106] Ibid.

[107] Ibid

[108] Bartlett's Familiar Quotations P.508 #8 Henrik Ibsen (1828-1906)

Made in the USA
Middletown, DE
24 August 2020

16288110R00177